Your Social Security Strategy

A Simple Guide to Timing, Taxes, and Retirement Income Decisions

Kayla Price

For additional educational resources, visit:

priceservicesgroup.com

Price Services Group, L.L.C.

info@priceservicesgroup.com | 1-866-648-1578

Printed in the United States of America. First Edition, 2026

Disclaimer

This guide is for educational purposes only.

It is not legal, tax, investment, Social Security, Medicare, or financial advice.

Nothing in this book, and no review described in it, creates an attorney-client relationship unless separately agreed in writing.

Social Security rules, tax laws, Medicare rules, and program limits may change.

Readers should consult qualified professionals before making decisions.

Price Services Group, L.L.C. is not affiliated with or endorsed by the Social Security Administration, Medicare, CMS, or any government agency.

Annuity and life insurance guarantees are based on the financial strength and claims-paying ability of the issuing carrier.

Examples in this book are simplified for educational use. Names, ages, family situations, and financial details in examples are fictional or generalized composites intended to illustrate planning concepts.

Although this 2026 edition reflects current information available at the time of writing, annual figures, claiming rules, premium amounts, earnings-test limits, taxable wage bases, and administrative procedures may be updated after publication.

A Note Before You Begin

Social Security looks simple from a distance. You work, you reach a certain age, and you start a monthly benefit. That is the version most people picture.

Then real life enters the conversation.

Your Social Security decision may connect to when you retire, whether you keep working, how much you withdraw from savings, how your spouse is protected, what Medicare may cost, how much of your benefit could be taxed, and what happens if one spouse dies first. A decision that appears to be only about one monthly check can affect the broader retirement picture for years.

If you have ever felt like everyone else understands Social Security better than you do, you are not alone. Many people are intelligent, responsible, and careful with money, yet still feel uncertain when it is time to make a claiming decision. Some readers are worried about making a mistake they cannot easily undo. Others are frustrated because online calculators give quick answers but not real context. Many simply want someone to help them sort through timing, taxes, Medicare, and income planning without making the process feel intimidating.

That is the purpose of this book.

This guide is written to help you understand the moving parts in plain language. It is meant to make the subject feel clearer, calmer, and more manageable. It is not meant to turn you into your own case analyst. General education and personal guidance are not the same thing.

Every Social Security decision happens inside a real household. That household has its own health history, cash-flow needs, tax picture, retirement savings, pension details, spousal concerns, survivor concerns, and comfort level with risk. Two people can be the same age and still need completely different strategies.

As you read, you will notice an idea repeated often: timing is personal. That repetition is intentional. The internet is full of broad opinions. Some say, "Claim early and get your money back." Others say, "Always wait until 70." Most real households need a more thoughtful conversation than either of those shortcuts can provide.

If this book helps you say, "I understand this better now, but I want to review my own situation before I decide," then it has done its job.

Table of Contents

Chapter One

Making Smarter Claiming Decisions

Timing, coordination, and the questions that matter most.

Kayla Price

Chapter 1: Social Security Without the Confusion

Social Security is one of the most important retirement income decisions many people will ever make, yet it is often treated like a simple form to complete. That is where confusion begins. People see a monthly estimate and assume the choice is mostly about whether to start now or later. In reality, the decision reaches into taxes, Medicare timing, survivor planning, and the way the rest of retirement income is organized.

For many households, Social Security is not just another payment. It is one of the few income sources that may continue for life and may receive cost-of-living adjustments over time. Because of that, the claiming decision can influence the pressure placed on savings, the amount of income a spouse may later depend on, and the flexibility a household has when markets or health circumstances change.

This chapter matters because it reframes the subject. Before talking about formulas or filing ages, it helps to understand why this decision deserves more attention than the average quick conversation gives it. When people slow down and see the ripple effects, they tend to make calmer and more intentional choices.

Simple Explanation

Many retirees focus on the gross monthly number. That is understandable. A benefit estimate feels concrete. It gives the impression that Social Security is a math problem with a single right answer. But the monthly number alone does not tell you what happens if you keep working, what taxes may apply, whether Medicare premiums may rise, or how your spouse could be affected later.

Another reason Social Security feels confusing is that people receive advice from many directions at once. Friends talk about what they did. Family members repeat what worked in a different decade. Online calculators produce neat-looking answers.

Headlines reward dramatic statements such as always claim early or always delay. None of those sources can see your household as a whole.

That is why general education is helpful but incomplete. Education gives you vocabulary. It helps you ask better questions. It shows you what issues may deserve attention. Personal guidance, on the other hand, helps sort through the facts that belong to your life rather than someone else's. The closer you get to retirement, the more important that distinction becomes.

Social Security also carries emotional weight. Some people are afraid the system will change and want to claim quickly. Some do not trust their health outlook. Some feel pressure because a spouse is waiting on their decision. Others worry about drawing down savings too fast if they wait. Those feelings are real. Good planning does not ignore them. It puts them into a bigger framework so the decision is not driven by one fear, one headline, or one isolated number.

Planning Perspective

One reason social security without the confusion deserves more space than a quick article or a short seminar comment is that the subject does not stay inside its own lane for very long. A person may begin by asking a straightforward question, then discover that the answer depends on work plans, marital status, spending needs, tax exposure, health concerns, or survivor priorities. That is why a chapter like this is not meant to overwhelm you with detail. It is meant to slow the conversation down enough for the important tradeoffs to become visible.

In real households, this topic usually shows up beside other retirement questions rather than by itself. Someone may be thinking about the household's expected retirement date and whether work income may continue, while also trying to sort out whether one spouse has a meaningfully larger earnings record than the other. Another household may be focused on how much of retirement income will come from savings, pensions, or part-time work and only later realize that Social Security timing is part of the same story. When pieces arrive in that order, the decision can feel more confusing than it really is. Often what is missing is not intelligence. It is simply a calm way to organize the moving parts.

This is also where broad guidance reaches its limit. A chart can teach. A rule of thumb can simplify. An online estimate can point you in the right direction. None of those tools can fully measure what retirement feels like inside one specific household. They do not know how cautious you are, how steady your income needs will be, how one spouse feels compared with the other, or how much flexibility you need if life changes. That is why education is helpful and still not the same thing as personal guidance.

Readers are often relieved when they realize they do not have to solve every part of this alone. You do not need to become your own Social Security office, tax preparer, Medicare analyst, and retirement-income engineer all at once. What you do need is enough understanding to recognize when a decision deserves a wider review. That is a very different goal from trying to self-manage every technical issue from scratch.

A thoughtful review usually changes the tone of the conversation. Instead of asking only, 'What is the biggest number?' people begin asking more useful questions. Which choice protects the household better over time? Which choice fits the way retirement income will actually be used? Which choice respects taxes, Medicare, and survivor concerns instead of discovering them later? Those are not dramatic questions. They are mature planning questions, and they often lead to steadier decisions.

Another reason to revisit this topic carefully is that retirement decisions usually unfold over time rather than all at once. A person may read a chapter like this today, file or delay months from now, and then have to revisit the same ideas after a work change, a health event, a market decline, a Medicare transition, or the loss of a spouse. Good education should still be useful when life moves.

That is one reason simple frameworks tend to serve people better than one-time slogans.

It is also worth noticing how often confidence grows when people stop asking for the perfect universal answer and start asking for the right answer for this season of life. The same household may need one strategy at sixty-two, a different strategy at sixty-six, and a different review again after Medicare begins or after one spouse dies. The rules matter, but the calendar of real life matters too. A thoughtful retirement review respects that timing instead of pretending every decision can be made once and ignored forever.

One final point is easy to underestimate: retirement decisions are rarely judged by math alone. They are lived out in monthly routines, family conversations, health changes, and the emotional experience of aging. A strategy that is technically impressive but constantly creates worry may not be the strongest strategy for that household. On the other hand, a strategy that supports steadier habits and clearer expectations may prove more durable over time. That is why practical fit belongs in the conversation right alongside rules and projections.

In that sense, planning around social security without the confusion is not only about information. It is also about alignment. The numbers matter. The rules matter. But the household's values matter too. Some people care deeply about future survivor protection. Some care most about present cash-flow relief. Some want to preserve flexibility because life has already taught them plans can change. A well-guided review makes room for those priorities without letting the conversation drift into guesswork.

That is why the most valuable outcome from this chapter is not memorizing one more rule. The real value is becoming better prepared for a personal review. When you can describe what concerns you, what facts you have, and what tradeoffs matter most, the next conversation becomes more productive. Clarity grows when the discussion moves from a generic topic to your actual retirement picture.

This is the place to separate the check from the strategy. A check is a dollar amount. A strategy asks how that amount supports the household, what it changes later, and what risks should not be ignored.

For most readers, the immediate goal is not to memorize Social Security. The goal is to understand why a personal review can prevent a narrow decision from becoming a long-term frustration.

A Couple Looking Only at the Check

Marcus and Denise both looked at their online Social Security accounts and immediately compared the estimated payments at age 62, full retirement age, and age 70. Marcus wanted the highest possible monthly check. Denise wanted to start earlier because she worried they would spend savings too quickly while waiting.

At first, the conversation seemed to be about which age gave the best value. After a fuller review, larger questions appeared. Marcus had the larger earnings record, which meant his claiming choice could affect Denise's later survivor income. They were also approaching Medicare decisions, and part of their retirement cash flow would come from IRAs with taxable withdrawals. Their Social Security timing could not be separated from the rest of the picture.

What looked like a simple disagreement over a monthly amount became a planning conversation about longevity, taxes, Medicare premiums, and survivor protection. They did not need a slogan. They needed context.

A Single Retiree With Too Many Opinions Around Her

Ellen planned to retire within a year. One friend told her she should claim at 62 because 'no one knows how long they have.' Another told her to wait until 70 because 'you always want the biggest check.' An online calculator gave her a break-even age but did not mention her part-time work or the tax impact of drawing from retirement accounts.

The pressure came from the idea that she was supposed to know the answer on her own. Once the conversation widened, Ellen could see that Social Security was only one piece of her income plan. The right question was not whether someone else's rule was correct. The right question was how her decision would interact with work, withdrawals, taxes, and her comfort level about future income.

That shift reduced anxiety. She no longer felt she had to guess between two extreme opinions. She could evaluate the decision in the context of her own retirement life.

What People Often Think

People often think Social Security is mostly about choosing an age from a chart. If 62 pays less and 70 pays more, the assumption is that the problem ends there.

People also often think the online estimate is close enough to the final answer. In many cases it is a helpful starting point, but it is not the same as a personal claiming analysis. It does not automatically account for how taxes, Medicare premiums, spousal concerns, or other income decisions fit together.

Another common belief is that there must be one best age for everyone. That belief sounds efficient, but it usually creates more confusion because real households are not identical.

What Actually Happens

What actually happens is that Social Security works like a hub in the middle of several other planning decisions. The claim date may affect how much income comes from savings first, how large future survivor benefits could be, how exposed the household is to tax surprises, and how secure the income plan feels later in retirement.

What actually happens is that people discover tradeoffs. Claiming early may reduce pressure in the near term but lock in a lower lifetime benefit. Waiting may increase the monthly amount but require a bridge from work or savings. Neither observation is automatically good or bad. It depends on the household.

What actually happens is that the strongest decision usually comes from reviewing the full retirement picture, not from isolating one Social Security estimate.

Where People Get Stuck

People often get stuck because the choice feels permanent. They know they may not have many do-overs, so they delay deciding or rely too heavily on simple rules.

They also get stuck when too many topics arrive at once. Retirement dates, Medicare enrollment, income planning, tax planning, and Social Security can all show up in the same season of life. Without a guide, the moving parts blur together.

Another place people get stuck is emotional. A couple may agree on their retirement goals but still react differently to uncertainty. One person wants the reassurance of income now. The other wants the comfort of a larger future benefit. That is not a failure. It simply means the conversation needs structure.

What We Typically Review Together

The household's expected retirement date and whether work income may continue.

Whether one spouse has a meaningfully larger earnings record than the other.

How much of retirement income will come from savings, pensions, or part-time work.

Whether taxes and Medicare premiums could change what the household actually keeps.

How the claiming choice may affect survivor income later.

What assumptions are coming from the internet, family, or friends rather than the household's own facts.

Social Security is connected to taxes, Medicare, and retirement income. That connection is worth repeating because it is where many otherwise thoughtful retirees get tripped up. Timing is personal. Online tools are starting points, not final answers. General advice is not the same as personal guidance. Claiming decisions can affect long-term income and survivor planning in ways that are easy to miss when the conversation stays too narrow.

Chapter Summary

Social Security matters because it is connected to much more than one monthly check. Timing decisions can ripple into taxes, Medicare, cash flow, and survivor planning.

The clearer you become on that point, the easier it is to see why broad advice is not enough. A decision this important deserves to be reviewed in the context of the whole retirement picture.

Once people understand why Social Security deserves careful attention, the next question is usually more practical: how is the benefit amount created in the first place? The next chapter explains the calculation in plain language without turning it into a textbook.

Chapter 2: How Your Benefit Is Calculated

This chapter matters because many claiming conversations become stressful simply because the benefit formula feels mysterious. When something feels mysterious, people either ignore it or give it more power than it deserves.

The good news is that you do not need to become a benefits technician to understand the basic structure. Once you know the main building blocks, the estimates you see online make more sense and the right questions become easier to ask.

Simple Explanation

At a high level, retirement benefits are built from your work history. Social Security looks at earnings that were subject to Social Security tax, adjusts those earnings through its formula, and then uses your highest 35 years of indexed earnings to calculate a base retirement amount.

That means your earnings record matters. If a year is missing, reported incorrectly, or lower than expected because of inconsistent work history, that can affect the benefit estimate. It also means people with fewer than 35 earning years may have zeros included in the calculation, which can lower the result.

People often hear about quarters or credits and assume that once they earn enough credits, the rest no longer matters. Credits matter for eligibility. In 2026, one quarter of coverage is earned with $1,890 of covered wages, and up to four credits can be earned during the year. But qualifying for benefits is not the same thing as maximizing them. The earnings history still affects the size of the benefit.

After the earnings history is processed, Social Security arrives at a primary insurance amount, often discussed as the full retirement age benefit. Full retirement age depends on birth year. For people attaining age 62 in 2026, full retirement age is 67. That full retirement age amount becomes the reference point for early or delayed claiming.

Claim earlier than full retirement age and the monthly benefit is reduced. Wait beyond full retirement age, up to age 70, and delayed retirement credits increase the monthly amount. In other words, the benefit estimate is not only about what you earned. It is also about when you start.

Planning Perspective

One reason how your benefit is calculated deserves more space than a quick article or a short seminar comment is that the subject does not stay inside its own lane for very long. A person may begin by asking a straightforward question, then discover that the answer depends on work plans, marital status, spending needs, tax exposure, health concerns, or survivor priorities. That is why a chapter like this is not meant to overwhelm you with detail. It is meant to slow the conversation down enough for the important tradeoffs to become visible.

In real households, this topic usually shows up beside other retirement questions rather than by itself. Someone may be thinking about the current Social Security earnings record and whether any years appear missing or inaccurate, while also trying to sort out whether the client has 35 years of covered earnings or may have low or zero years in the formula. Another household may be focused on how the projected full retirement age benefit compares with the age 62 and age 70 estimates and only later realize that Social Security timing is part of the same story. When pieces arrive in that order, the decision can feel more confusing than it really is. Often what is missing is not intelligence. It is simply a calm way to organize the moving parts.

This is also where broad guidance reaches its limit. A chart can teach. A rule of thumb can simplify. An online estimate can point you in the right direction. None of those tools can fully measure what retirement feels like inside one specific household. They do not know how cautious you are, how steady your income needs will be, how one spouse feels compared with the other, or how much flexibility you need if life changes. That is why education is helpful and still not the same thing as personal guidance.

Readers are often relieved when they realize they do not have to solve every part of this alone. You do not need to become your own Social Security office, tax preparer, Medicare analyst, and retirement-income engineer all at once. What you do need is enough understanding to recognize when a decision deserves a wider review. That is a very different goal from trying to self-manage every technical issue from scratch.

A thoughtful review usually changes the tone of the conversation. Instead of asking only, 'What is the biggest number?' people begin asking more useful questions. Which choice protects the household better over time? Which choice fits the way retirement income will actually be used? Which choice respects taxes, Medicare, and survivor concerns instead of discovering them later? Those are not dramatic questions. They are mature planning questions, and they often lead to steadier decisions.

Another reason to revisit this topic carefully is that retirement decisions usually unfold over time rather than all at once. A person may read a chapter like this today, file or delay months from now, and then have to revisit the same ideas after a work change, a health event, a market decline, a Medicare transition, or the loss of a spouse. Good education should still be useful when life moves. That is one reason simple frameworks tend to serve people better than one-time slogans.

It is also worth noticing how often confidence grows when people stop asking for the perfect universal answer and start asking for the right answer for this season of life. The same household may need one strategy at sixty-two, a different strategy at sixty-six, and a different review again after Medicare begins or after one spouse dies. The rules matter, but the calendar of real life matters too. A thoughtful retirement review respects that timing instead of pretending every decision can be made once and ignored forever.

One final point is easy to underestimate: retirement decisions are rarely judged by math alone. They are lived out in monthly routines, family conversations, health changes, and the emotional experience of aging. A strategy that is technically impressive but constantly creates worry may not be the strongest strategy for that household. On the other hand, a strategy that supports steadier habits and clearer expectations may prove more durable over time. That is why practical fit belongs in the conversation right alongside rules and projections.

In that sense, planning around how your benefit is calculated is not only about information. It is also about alignment. The numbers matter. The rules matter. But the household's values matter too. Some people care deeply about future survivor protection. Some care most about present cash-flow relief. Some want to preserve flexibility because life has already taught them plans can change. A well-guided review makes room for those priorities without letting the conversation drift into guesswork.

That is why the most valuable outcome from this chapter is not memorizing one more rule. The real value is becoming better prepared for a personal review. When you can describe what concerns you, what facts you have, and what tradeoffs matter most, the next conversation becomes more productive. Clarity grows when the discussion moves from a generic topic to your actual retirement picture.

The calculation matters because your benefit estimate is only as accurate as the work record behind it. A missing year, an incorrect earnings record, or a few lower earning years can change expectations.

This is also why reviewing the Social Security statement before a planning conversation is helpful. It gives the conversation a real starting point instead of relying on memory or guesses.

A Strong Earner With Missing Years

Harold assumed his benefit would be near the top of the range because he had a long career with several strong earning years. During a review, he realized that a few years early in his work life were either low or missing from the record used in his estimate.

Those years did not erase decades of work, but they still mattered because Social Security uses the highest 35 years. Replacing a zero or a very low year can make a difference. Even when a claiming decision is still several years away, confirming the earnings record can be worthwhile.

The lesson was simple: do not confuse a rough estimate with a completed review. Sometimes the first useful step is simply verifying the foundation.

A Reader Who Thought Credits Were the Whole Story

Patricia knew she had enough credits to qualify, so she assumed her benefit would be close to a friend's. But the two had very different earnings histories. Patricia spent many years out of the workforce helping family members, while her friend had a long stretch of higher covered earnings.

Eligibility opened the door. It did not determine the size of the room. Once Patricia understood that the formula looks at work history and not just credits, the estimate felt less confusing.

That clarity also helped her ask a better question. Instead of asking only, 'Do I qualify?' she began asking, 'How does my own record shape the range of realistic claiming options?'

What People Often Think

People often think benefits are based on their last salary or their best few years. That is not how the retirement benefit is built.

People also often think getting enough credits means they have done the important part. Credits are important, but they mainly tell you whether you have earned the right to qualify.

Another common assumption is that the estimate shown at one age is fixed forever, when in reality work, updated earnings, and claiming age can still change the outcome.

What Actually Happens

What actually happens is that the benefit is shaped by a long history, not a single paycheck. The highest 35 years matter, and lower years can still affect the average.

What actually happens is that annual numbers change. In 2026 the maximum taxable earnings base for Social Security is $184,500, and the maximum retirement benefit for a worker retiring at full retirement age is listed by SSA as $4,152 per month. Those numbers help frame the system, but they are not planning shortcuts by themselves. Annual figures and program rules can change. Verify current numbers and program details before making decisions.

What actually happens is that the full retirement age amount becomes the benchmark for future claiming discussions. Once people understand that benchmark, early claiming reductions and delayed credits feel much easier to follow.

Where People Get Stuck

People get stuck when they see several estimates at different ages and do not know which one is the 'real' number. The truth is that they are all estimates built on different filing assumptions.

They also get stuck when they try to reverse-engineer the federal formula line by line. That level of detail may be interesting, but it is not always helpful. Most readers do better by understanding the broad mechanics and then reviewing their own records carefully.

Another sticking point is confidence. Some people assume the government record must be perfect. Others assume it is probably wrong. A measured review is better than either extreme.

What We Typically Review Together

The current Social Security earnings record and whether any years appear missing or inaccurate.

Whether the client has 35 years of covered earnings or may have low or zero years in the formula.

How the projected full retirement age benefit compares with the age 62 and age 70 estimates.

Whether ongoing work could still replace lower earnings years before claiming.

How much confidence the household should place in a general estimate versus a personal review.

Social Security is connected to taxes, Medicare, and retirement income. That connection is worth repeating because it is where many otherwise thoughtful retirees get tripped up. Timing is personal. Online tools are starting points, not final answers. General advice is not the same as personal guidance. Claiming decisions can affect long-term income and survivor planning in ways that are easy to miss when the conversation stays too narrow.

Chapter Summary

Your benefit is based on more than eligibility alone. Earnings history, highest 35 years, and claiming age all matter.

You do not need to memorize the full formula to make a strong decision, but you do need to understand what the estimate is built on and verify that the foundation is sound.

Once the benefit formula is less intimidating, the next practical question is timing. The next chapter walks through the main claiming windows and the tradeoffs attached to each one.

Chapter 3: When You Can Claim

This chapter matters because timing is where most people first feel the weight of the decision. It is one thing to know a benefit exists. It is another to decide when to turn it on.

The common ages people hear about are 62, full retirement age, and 70. Those ages are useful markers, but they should be understood as decision points with tradeoffs rather than as automatic answers.

Simple Explanation

Age 62 is the earliest age many people can claim retirement benefits. That early access can feel appealing, especially for those who want income sooner, are leaving work earlier than expected, or want to reduce withdrawals from savings. The tradeoff is that the monthly benefit is reduced for claiming before full retirement age.

Full retirement age is the age at which you are eligible for your unreduced retirement benefit based on your work record. For people born in 1960 or later, full retirement age is 67. For some older birth years, the age is between 66 and 67. That full retirement age amount often becomes the anchor point in planning discussions.

Age 70 is the latest point at which delayed retirement credits increase the retirement benefit. Waiting from full retirement age to 70 can significantly raise the monthly amount, but waiting also means the household needs another source of income during the delay period.

These ages are not simply better or worse versions of each other. They each fit different circumstances. Claiming earlier may create flexibility now. Claiming later may create stronger income later. The important point is not to confuse a larger benefit with a universally better decision or a smaller benefit with a universally bad one.

This is also a good place to remember that online tools are starting points. They can show a range of estimates by age, and that is useful. But they do not decide which tradeoff fits your family.

Planning Perspective

One reason when you can claim deserves more space than a quick article or a short seminar comment is that the subject does not stay inside its own lane for very long. A person may begin by asking a straightforward question, then discover that the answer depends on work plans, marital status, spending needs, tax exposure, health concerns, or survivor priorities. That is why a chapter like this is not meant to overwhelm you with detail. It is meant to slow the conversation down enough for the important tradeoffs to become visible.

In real households, this topic usually shows up beside other retirement questions rather than by itself. Someone may be thinking about the estimated benefit at age 62, full retirement age, and age 70, while also trying to sort out whether a larger benefit later would meaningfully improve household stability or survivor protection. Another household may be focused on Whether the household can fund the gap if claiming is delayed and only later realize that Social Security timing is part of the same story. When pieces arrive in that order, the decision can feel more confusing than it really is. Often what is missing is not intelligence. It is simply a calm way to organize the moving parts.

This is also where broad guidance reaches its limit. A chart can teach. A rule of thumb can simplify. An online estimate can point you in the right direction. None of those tools can fully measure what retirement feels like inside one specific household. They do not know how cautious you are, how steady your income needs will be, how one spouse feels compared with the other, or how much flexibility you need if life changes. That is why education is helpful and still not the same thing as personal guidance.

Readers are often relieved when they realize they do not have to solve every part of this alone. You do not need to become your own Social Security office, tax preparer, Medicare analyst, and retirement-income engineer all at once. What you do need is enough understanding to recognize when a decision deserves a wider review. That is a very different goal from trying to self-manage every technical issue from scratch.

A thoughtful review usually changes the tone of the conversation. Instead of asking only, 'What is the biggest number?' people begin asking more useful questions. Which choice protects the household better over time? Which choice fits the way retirement income will actually be used? Which choice respects taxes, Medicare, and survivor concerns instead of discovering them later? Those are not dramatic questions. They are mature planning questions, and they often lead to steadier decisions.

Another reason to revisit this topic carefully is that retirement decisions usually unfold over time rather than all at once. A person may read a chapter like this today, file or delay months from now, and then have to revisit the same ideas after a work change, a health event, a market decline, a Medicare transition, or the loss of a spouse. Good education should still be useful when life moves. That is one reason simple frameworks tend to serve people better than one-time slogans.

It is also worth noticing how often confidence grows when people stop asking for the perfect universal answer and start asking for the right answer for this season of life. The same household may need one strategy at sixty-two, a different strategy at sixty-six, and a different review again after Medicare begins or after one spouse dies. The rules matter, but the calendar of real life matters too. A thoughtful retirement review respects that timing instead of pretending every decision can be made once and ignored forever.

One final point is easy to underestimate: retirement decisions are rarely judged by math alone. They are lived out in monthly routines, family conversations, health changes, and the emotional

experience of aging. A strategy that is technically impressive but constantly creates worry may not be the strongest strategy for that household. On the other hand, a strategy that supports steadier habits and clearer expectations may prove more durable over time. That is why practical fit belongs in the conversation right alongside rules and projections.

In that sense, planning around when you can claim is not only about information. It is also about alignment. The numbers matter. The rules matter. But the household's values matter too. Some people care deeply about future survivor protection. Some care most about present cash-flow relief. Some want to preserve flexibility because life has already taught them plans can change. A well-guided review makes room for those priorities without letting the conversation drift into guesswork.

That is why the most valuable outcome from this chapter is not memorizing one more rule. The real value is becoming better prepared for a personal review. When you can describe what concerns you, what facts you have, and what tradeoffs matter most, the next conversation becomes more productive. Clarity grows when the discussion moves from a generic topic to your actual retirement picture.

The claiming ages are easy to list but not always easy to choose. The right age depends on how income, health, work, spouse protection, and savings fit together.

A person who only sees the chart may think the decision is finished. A household that reviews the whole picture often sees tradeoffs the chart did not show.

Leaving Work Earlier Than Planned

Sandra expected to work until 67, but a layoff at 63 changed the conversation. She looked at claiming immediately because it felt safer than drawing from savings.

That reaction made sense, but it was only the first layer. A better review looked at whether she would return to part-time work, how much she had in retirement accounts, what taxes might apply, and whether waiting could create a more stable long-term income stream. The question was not whether claiming at 63 was good or bad. The question was whether it fit her broader situation.

Without that broader review, she might have treated a temporary disruption like a permanent strategy.

Choosing Between Full Retirement Age and 70

James reached full retirement age and assumed that filing then was the balanced choice simply because it sounded moderate. His spouse asked whether waiting longer might help the household later.

That led to a more thoughtful discussion. James had the higher earnings record, and his spouse would likely depend on the larger benefit if he died first. Delaying was not only about his own monthly income. It could also strengthen potential survivor income.

In that case, the jump from full retirement age to 70 was not just a personal preference. It was part of a couple's protection strategy.

What People Often Think

People often think age 62 is the 'risky' choice and age 70 is the 'smart' choice. That may be true in some cases, but it is not a rule that can be safely applied to everyone.

Others think full retirement age is the obvious compromise and therefore must be right. Sometimes it is. Sometimes it is simply the most familiar option rather than the most intentional one.

Another common belief is that once someone sees the estimates at each age, the decision should be obvious. Real households rarely feel that simple.

What Actually Happens

What actually happens is that each filing age changes the shape of the retirement plan. Earlier claiming can reduce the need to draw from other assets right away. Delayed claiming can create more guaranteed monthly income later.

What actually happens is that the best age depends on issues outside the Social Security statement. Health, longevity expectations, marital status, work plans, taxes, and income needs all matter.

What actually happens is that the claiming-age conversation often opens the door to a broader review. It becomes clear that the filing choice should be coordinated with retirement income planning, not treated in isolation.

Where People Get Stuck

People get stuck when they try to find a perfect answer before reviewing the rest of retirement. That usually creates delay rather than clarity.

They also get stuck when they hear strong opinions from people they trust. Advice from friends or relatives may be sincere, but it reflects someone else's facts, not yours.

Another sticking point is uncertainty about work. If retirement timing is still changing, the Social Security decision may feel hard to lock down. That is exactly why a review should stay flexible rather than formula-driven.

What We Typically Review Together

The estimated benefit at age 62, full retirement age, and age 70.

Whether a larger benefit later would meaningfully improve household stability or survivor protection.

Whether the household can fund the gap if claiming is delayed.

How work, taxes, Medicare enrollment, and other income sources influence the timing choice.

What emotional concerns are driving the decision in the background.

Social Security is connected to taxes, Medicare, and retirement income. That connection is worth repeating because it is where many otherwise thoughtful retirees get tripped up. Timing is personal. Online tools are starting points, not final answers. General advice is not the same as personal guidance. Claiming decisions can affect long-term income and survivor planning in ways that are easy to miss when the conversation stays too narrow.

Chapter Summary

The main claiming windows are easy to name, but they are not one-size-fits-all answers. Each age changes the tradeoffs in a different way.

A simple estimate chart can begin the conversation, but it should not end it.

If you would like help reviewing how Social Security fits into your broader retirement picture, you can schedule a personalized Social Security review at:

https://host.safemsngr.com/widget/bookings/psgss

Chapter 4: When Should You Claim?

This chapter matters because the claiming decision is where education becomes personal. Many people can understand the rules and still feel uncertain about applying them to their own life.

When should you claim? The honest answer is that it depends on more than one number and more than one year of life. A stronger answer comes from looking at the decision from several angles at once.

Simple Explanation

One concept that often appears in claiming conversations is break-even analysis. This compares the value of starting earlier with the value of receiving a larger payment later. The concept can be useful because it shows that waiting is not free and claiming early is not costless either.

But break-even analysis is not the whole decision. It usually assumes a simplified life path and may ignore taxes, survivor benefits, spousal concerns, investment withdrawals, health changes, and peace of mind. It is a tool, not a conclusion.

Health matters, but it should be handled carefully. People sometimes make permanent claiming decisions based on fear, one medical event, or a family history that may not fully reflect their own situation. Health can absolutely influence timing, yet it should be discussed with humility and context rather than as a dramatic prediction.

Longevity matters too. The longer someone lives, the more valuable a larger monthly benefit may become. For couples, longevity planning often becomes survivor planning. The higher earner's decision can later affect the income that remains for the surviving spouse.

Income need is another major factor. Some people delay because they can. Others claim earlier because they need the money.

Neither reality should be judged. The important thing is to understand the long-term effect of the decision and make sure short-term income choices do not accidentally undermine long-term stability.

Retirement savings also play a role. In some households, carefully using savings for a few years can support delaying benefits and strengthening guaranteed lifetime income. In other households, preserving savings may be more important than delaying. The better decision is usually the one that fits the full plan, not the one that wins a theoretical debate.

Planning Perspective

One reason when should you claim? deserves more space than a quick article or a short seminar comment is that the subject does not stay inside its own lane for very long. A person may begin by asking a straightforward question, then discover that the answer depends on work plans, marital status, spending needs, tax exposure, health concerns, or survivor priorities. That is why a chapter like this is not meant to overwhelm you with detail. It is meant to slow the conversation down enough for the important tradeoffs to become visible.

In real households, this topic usually shows up beside other retirement questions rather than by itself. Someone may be thinking about Expected income needs in the early retirement years and later retirement years, while also trying to sort out How a delay or an early claim changes withdrawals from savings or pensions. Another household may be focused on Whether one spouse's benefit is important for future survivor income and only later realize that Social Security timing is part of the same story. When pieces arrive in that order, the decision can feel more confusing than it really is. Often what is missing is not intelligence. It is simply a calm way to organize the moving parts.

This is also where broad guidance reaches its limit. A chart can teach. A rule of thumb can simplify. An online estimate can point you in the right direction. None of those tools can fully measure what retirement feels like inside one specific household. They do not know how cautious you are, how steady your income needs will be, how one spouse feels compared with the other, or how much flexibility you need if life changes. That is why education is helpful and still not the same thing as personal guidance.

Readers are often relieved when they realize they do not have to solve every part of this alone. You do not need to become your own Social Security office, tax preparer, Medicare analyst, and retirement-income engineer all at once. What you do need is enough understanding to recognize when a decision deserves a wider review. That is a very different goal from trying to self-manage every technical issue from scratch.

A thoughtful review usually changes the tone of the conversation. Instead of asking only, 'What is the biggest number?' people begin asking more useful questions. Which choice protects the household better over time? Which choice fits the way retirement income will actually be used? Which choice respects taxes, Medicare, and survivor concerns instead of discovering them later? Those are not dramatic questions. They are mature planning questions, and they often lead to steadier decisions.

Another reason to revisit this topic carefully is that retirement decisions usually unfold over time rather than all at once. A person may read a chapter like this today, file or delay months from now, and then have to revisit the same ideas after a work change, a health event, a market decline, a Medicare transition, or the loss of a spouse. Good education should still be useful when life moves. That is one reason simple frameworks tend to serve people better than one-time slogans.

It is also worth noticing how often confidence grows when people stop asking for the perfect universal answer and start asking for the right answer for this season of life. The same household may need one strategy at sixty-two, a different strategy at sixty-six, and a different review again after Medicare begins or after one spouse dies. The rules matter, but the calendar of real life matters too. A thoughtful retirement review respects that timing instead of pretending every decision can be made once and ignored forever.

One final point is easy to underestimate: retirement decisions are rarely judged by math alone. They are lived out in monthly routines, family conversations, health changes, and the emotional experience of aging. A strategy that is technically impressive but constantly creates worry may not be the strongest strategy for that household. On the other hand, a strategy that supports steadier habits and clearer expectations may prove more durable over time. That is why practical fit belongs in the conversation right alongside rules and projections.

In that sense, planning around when should you claim? is not only about information. It is also about alignment. The numbers matter. The rules matter. But the household's values matter too. Some people care deeply about future survivor protection. Some care most about present cash-flow relief. Some want to preserve flexibility because life has already taught them plans can change. A well-guided review makes room for those priorities without letting the conversation drift into guesswork.

That is why the most valuable outcome from this chapter is not memorizing one more rule. The real value is becoming better prepared for a personal review. When you can describe what concerns you, what facts you have, and what tradeoffs matter most, the next conversation becomes more productive. Clarity grows when the discussion moves from a generic topic to your actual retirement picture.

This is where the decision becomes personal. A higher monthly benefit can be attractive, but the household must also consider the income bridge required to wait.

The strongest answer is rarely based on one calculation. It comes from comparing the numbers with the reality of cash flow, health, spouse needs, and comfort level.

A Healthy Couple With a Survivor Concern

Victor and Laura entered retirement with solid savings and no immediate need for Social Security income. Victor's benefit was materially higher than Laura's. Their first instinct was to claim together once they both stopped working simply to make the process feel complete.

A review changed the conversation. If Victor delayed, the household would likely receive a larger monthly amount later, and that larger amount could matter if Laura outlived him. Their decision was not just about early retirement cash flow. It was about protecting the spouse who might one day live on one check instead of two.

For them, waiting was not an abstract optimization exercise. It was part of a household protection strategy.

A Retiree With Immediate Income Pressure

Carol wanted to delay until 70 because she had heard that waiting always wins. But her pension was modest, her part-time work was ending, and heavy withdrawals from savings would have been required if she delayed several more years.

In her case, the best decision had to respect present cash flow, not just future benefit size. Claiming earlier did not mean she was making a weak choice. It meant she was aligning the strategy with the income pressure she actually faced.

The lesson was that good planning respects reality. Strong advice should help people make clearer decisions, not push them into a version of retirement that does not fit.

What People Often Think

People often think break-even age gives the answer. It gives a lens, not the final answer.

They also often think the claiming decision is mostly about individual life expectancy. That matters, but for married couples the surviving spouse may be just as important as the person claiming.

Another common belief is that if delaying increases the monthly amount, then everyone who can technically wait should wait. That ignores cash flow, emotional comfort, and the rest of the retirement plan.

What Actually Happens

What actually happens is that the right claiming age comes from balancing tradeoffs, not solving one equation. Health, longevity, work, taxes, retirement accounts, spouse needs, and survivor protection all pull on the choice.

What actually happens is that households need different kinds of confidence. Some people need stronger future income. Some need current income now. Some need to protect the surviving spouse. Some need to coordinate Social Security with a careful withdrawal plan.

What actually happens is that the best decision often feels less dramatic than expected. It is usually the decision that still makes sense after the rest of the retirement picture is laid on the table.

Where People Get Stuck

People get stuck when they want certainty about an uncertain future. No one can know exact lifespan, exact market returns, future tax law, or every health event ahead of time.

They also get stuck when they compare themselves to people in very different financial situations. Advice that fits a dual-income couple with strong assets may not fit a single retiree who needs income sooner.

Another place people stall is decision fatigue. By the time retirement arrives, they may already be making decisions about Medicare, work, debt, housing, and estate documents. Social Security can become one more important choice in a crowded season.

What We Typically Review Together

Expected income needs in the early retirement years and later retirement years.

How a delay or an early claim changes withdrawals from savings or pensions.

Whether one spouse's benefit is important for future survivor income.

How taxes and Medicare premiums may change under different claiming-and-withdrawal combinations.

Whether the household values flexibility today, larger guaranteed income later, or a balance of both.

Social Security is connected to taxes, Medicare, and retirement income. That connection is worth repeating because it is where many otherwise thoughtful retirees get tripped up. Timing is personal. Online tools are starting points, not final answers. General advice is not the same as personal guidance. Claiming decisions can affect long-term income and survivor planning in ways that are easy to miss when the conversation stays too narrow.

Chapter Summary

Break-even analysis can help, but it should not dominate the decision. Claiming is personal because retirement itself is personal.

A confident choice usually comes from coordinating Social Security with the rest of the household plan rather than trying to solve the question in isolation.

Timing decisions are easier when people also understand how work may affect benefits. The next chapter explains why many people are surprised when they claim and continue earning income at the same time.

Chapter 5: Working While Receiving Social Security

This chapter matters because many people do not move from full-time work to full retirement in one clean step. Some keep working by choice. Some return to work later. Some reduce hours gradually. Social Security and work often overlap.

That overlap can create surprises, especially when benefits are claimed before full retirement age. Understanding the earnings rules ahead of time can prevent a lot of unnecessary frustration.

Simple Explanation

If you claim retirement benefits before full retirement age and continue working, Social Security may withhold part of the benefit if earnings exceed the annual earnings-test limit. In 2026, the exempt amount for someone under full retirement age for the entire year is $24,480. Social Security withholds $1 in benefits for every $2 of earnings above that amount.

In the year you reach full retirement age, a higher limit applies to earnings before the month you reach that age. In 2026 that higher exempt amount is $65,160, and the withholding formula is $1 for every $3 above the limit. Beginning with the month full retirement age is reached, the earnings test no longer applies.

These numbers are important, but so is the language around them. Benefits are not always 'lost forever' in the way people fear. Social Security may later adjust the monthly amount to account for months in which benefits were withheld. Still, the short-term cash-flow surprise can be very real, which is why planning matters. Annual figures and program rules can change. Verify current numbers and program details before making decisions.

Another source of confusion is that people may think any income causes a problem. In reality, the details depend on the type of earnings and the timing. That is one more reason not to assume a friend's experience matches your own.

Planning Perspective

One reason working while receiving social security deserves more space than a quick article or a short seminar comment is that the subject does not stay inside its own lane for very long. A person may begin by asking a straightforward question, then discover that the answer depends on work plans, marital status, spending needs, tax exposure, health concerns, or survivor priorities. That is why a chapter like this is not meant to overwhelm you with detail. It is meant to slow the conversation down enough for the important tradeoffs to become visible.

In real households, this topic usually shows up beside other retirement questions rather than by itself. Someone may be thinking about Expected wages or self-employment income before full retirement age, while also trying to sort out whether retirement is truly complete or simply shifting into part-time work. Another household may be focused on The likely effect of earnings-test withholding on monthly cash flow and only later realize that Social Security timing is part of the same story. When pieces arrive in that order, the decision can feel more confusing than it really is. Often what is missing is not intelligence. It is simply a calm way to organize the moving parts.

This is also where broad guidance reaches its limit. A chart can teach. A rule of thumb can simplify. An online estimate can point you in the right direction. None of those tools can fully measure what retirement feels like inside one specific household. They do not know how cautious you are, how steady your income needs will be, how one spouse feels compared with the other, or how much flexibility you need if life changes. That is why education is helpful and still not the same thing as personal guidance.

Readers are often relieved when they realize they do not have to solve every part of this alone. You do not need to become your own Social Security office, tax preparer, Medicare analyst, and retirement-income engineer all at once. What you do need is enough understanding to recognize when a decision deserves a wider review. That is a very different goal from trying to self-manage every technical issue from scratch.

A thoughtful review usually changes the tone of the conversation. Instead of asking only, 'What is the biggest number?' people begin asking more useful questions. Which choice protects the household better over time? Which choice fits the way retirement income will actually be used? Which choice respects taxes, Medicare, and survivor concerns instead of discovering them later? Those are not dramatic questions. They are mature planning questions, and they often lead to steadier decisions.

Another reason to revisit this topic carefully is that retirement decisions usually unfold over time rather than all at once. A person may read a chapter like this today, file or delay months from now, and then have to revisit the same ideas after a work change, a health event, a market decline, a Medicare transition, or the loss of a spouse. Good education should still be useful when life moves. That is one reason simple frameworks tend to serve people better than one-time slogans.

It is also worth noticing how often confidence grows when people stop asking for the perfect universal answer and start asking for the right answer for this season of life. The same household may need one strategy at sixty-two, a different strategy at sixty-six, and a different review again after Medicare begins or after one spouse dies. The rules matter, but the calendar of real life matters too. A thoughtful retirement review respects that timing instead of pretending every decision can be made once and ignored forever.

One final point is easy to underestimate: retirement decisions are rarely judged by math alone. They are lived out in monthly routines, family conversations, health changes, and the emotional experience of aging. A strategy that is technically impressive but constantly creates worry may not be the strongest strategy for that household. On the other hand, a strategy that supports steadier habits and clearer expectations may prove more durable over time.

That is why practical fit belongs in the conversation right alongside rules and projections.

In that sense, planning around working while receiving social security is not only about information. It is also about alignment. The numbers matter. The rules matter. But the household's values matter too. Some people care deeply about future survivor protection. Some care most about present cash-flow relief. Some want to preserve flexibility because life has already taught them plans can change. A well-guided review makes room for those priorities without letting the conversation drift into guesswork.

That is why the most valuable outcome from this chapter is not memorizing one more rule. The real value is becoming better prepared for a personal review. When you can describe what concerns you, what facts you have, and what tradeoffs matter most, the next conversation becomes more productive. Clarity grows when the discussion moves from a generic topic to your actual retirement picture.

Working while receiving benefits can be perfectly reasonable, but it should not be an accidental surprise. Earnings limits, tax exposure, and timing can all affect how smooth the decision feels.

A short review before filing can help avoid the feeling of doing the right thing and then being surprised by withheld benefits or unexpected tax results.

Claiming at 62 and Keeping a Busy Schedule

Renee claimed benefits at 62 because she wanted the flexibility to reduce her full-time workload. Soon after, she accepted consulting work that paid more than expected.

She was surprised to learn that earnings above the limit could trigger withholding. The problem was not that she had done something wrong. The problem was that she made the claiming decision without fully coordinating it with expected work income.

A better review would have helped her compare two paths: claim now and manage the earnings test carefully, or delay claiming until the work transition was clearer.

Returning to Work After Claiming

Michael claimed early after leaving a long-term job. Six months later, a former employer invited him back in a part-time role that gradually became more substantial.

He thought the job would simply add to his retirement income. Instead, it reopened questions about earnings limits, withholding, and whether his original filing decision still fit the plan. The situation was manageable, but it was no longer simple.

This kind of story is common. Retirement is often phased, not abrupt. A claiming decision should leave room for that reality.

What People Often Think

People often think once they claim, they can earn whatever they want and nothing changes. That is not true before full retirement age.

Others think withholding means the government has permanently taken their benefit away. The truth is more nuanced than that.

Another common belief is that the earnings test is a minor technicality that can be dealt with later. In practice, it can materially affect short-term cash flow and should be part of the initial decision.

What Actually Happens

What actually happens is that working while claiming early can change what arrives in the mailbox or bank account. A household expecting the full estimated payment may be caught off guard if withholding occurs.

What actually happens is that the earnings test becomes part of the broader timing question. If work will continue meaningfully, waiting may be cleaner in some cases. In other cases, early claiming still makes sense, but only after the work income is reviewed honestly.

What actually happens is that flexible retirement calls for flexible planning. The more likely it is that work income will continue, the more important it becomes to connect the Social Security decision to the real work plan.

Where People Get Stuck

People get stuck because they are not fully retired but do not want to keep delaying the benefit decision.

They also get stuck when self-employment or uneven consulting income makes earnings harder to predict. Planning feels easy with a fixed salary and much harder with variable work.

Another sticking point is pride. Some people hesitate to ask basic questions because they think they should already know how the rule works. In truth, this is one of the most common areas of confusion.

What We Typically Review Together

Expected wages or self-employment income before full retirement age.

Whether retirement is truly complete or simply shifting into part-time work.

The likely effect of earnings-test withholding on monthly cash flow.

Whether delaying the claim could reduce complexity or strengthen the long-term plan.

How work income affects taxes, savings withdrawals, and Medicare timing.

Social Security is connected to taxes, Medicare, and retirement income. That connection is worth repeating because it is where many otherwise thoughtful retirees get tripped up. Timing is personal. Online tools are starting points, not final answers. General advice is not the same as personal guidance. Claiming decisions can affect long-term income and survivor planning in ways that are easy to miss when the conversation stays too narrow.

Chapter Summary

Working while receiving Social Security is common, but it needs to be planned for, especially before full retirement age.

The earnings test does not make early claiming impossible. It simply makes coordination more important.

Once people understand that the stated benefit and the deposited benefit are not always the same, it becomes easier to discuss taxes and Medicare. The next chapter explains why what you receive is not always what you keep.

Chapter 6: Taxes, Medicare, and Hidden Costs

This chapter matters because many people plan around the Social Security amount they expect to receive and are caught off guard by what actually remains after taxes and Medicare costs are factored in.

The phrase to remember is simple: what you receive is not always what you keep. That is not meant to create fear. It is meant to create realism.

Simple Explanation

A portion of Social Security benefits may be taxable at the federal level depending on provisional income, sometimes called combined income. The commonly referenced federal thresholds often used in basic planning are $25,000 and $34,000 for single filers, and $32,000 and $44,000 for married couples filing jointly. Depending on the result, up to 50 percent or up to 85 percent of benefits may be included in taxable income.

That does not mean 50 percent or 85 percent is automatically taxed away. It means that portion of benefits becomes subject to the tax calculation. Even so, the impact can be meaningful when Social Security is layered on top of IRA withdrawals, pension income, work income, or other taxable sources.

Medicare also belongs in this conversation. Many people enroll in Medicare around retirement and assume the standard premium is the end of the story. In 2026 the standard Medicare Part B premium is $202.90 per month, with an annual deductible of $283. Higher-income households may pay more through income-related monthly adjustment amounts, often called IRMAA.

For 2026, Medicare Part B IRMAA begins above modified adjusted gross income of $109,000 for an individual return and $218,000 for a joint return, with higher tiers above that. Part D income-related adjustments can also apply. That means a claiming strategy and withdrawal strategy may influence not only taxes but also Medicare premium levels.

This is why Social Security cannot be separated from retirement income planning. A larger income year may help in one way and create pressure in another. Good planning does not chase a single line item. It studies the interaction.

Important Medicare Premium Note

Higher-income households may pay more for Medicare Part B and Part D through IRMAA. For 2026, those added costs generally begin when modified adjusted gross income is above $109,000 for an individual return or $218,000 for a joint return.

Just as important, Medicare usually looks back to tax information from two years earlier. That means a larger-income year can affect premiums later even if current income has already fallen. If income later dropped because of a qualifying life-changing event, that may be a reason to review whether a lower determination can be requested.

Planning Perspective

One reason taxes, medicare, and hidden costs deserves more space than a quick article or a short seminar comment is that the subject does not stay inside its own lane for very long. A person may begin by asking a straightforward question, then discover that the answer depends on work plans, marital status, spending needs, tax exposure, health concerns, or survivor priorities. That is why a chapter like this is not meant to overwhelm you with detail. It is meant to slow the conversation down enough for the important tradeoffs to become visible.

In real households, this topic usually shows up beside other retirement questions rather than by itself. Someone may be thinking about Tax filing status and the likely mix of taxable and non-taxable retirement income sources, while also trying to sort out whether IRA withdrawals, pensions, or work income could change the taxation of benefits. Another household may be focused on Current or expected Medicare enrollment and whether IRMAA may become a concern and only later realize that Social Security timing is part of the same story. When pieces arrive in that order, the decision can feel more confusing than it really is. Often what is missing is not intelligence. It is simply a calm way to organize the moving parts.

This is also where broad guidance reaches its limit. A chart can teach. A rule of thumb can simplify. An online estimate can point you in the right direction. None of those tools can fully measure what retirement feels like inside one specific household. They do not know how cautious you are, how steady your income needs will be, how one spouse feels compared with the other, or how much flexibility you need if life changes. That is why education is helpful and still not the same thing as personal guidance.

Readers are often relieved when they realize they do not have to solve every part of this alone. You do not need to become your own Social Security office, tax preparer, Medicare analyst, and retirement-income engineer all at once. What you do need is enough understanding to recognize when a decision deserves a wider review. That is a very different goal from trying to self-manage every technical issue from scratch.

A thoughtful review usually changes the tone of the conversation. Instead of asking only, 'What is the biggest number?' people begin asking more useful questions. Which choice protects the household better over time? Which choice fits the way retirement income will actually be used? Which choice respects taxes, Medicare, and survivor concerns instead of discovering them later? Those are not dramatic questions. They are mature planning questions, and they often lead to steadier decisions.

Another reason to revisit this topic carefully is that retirement decisions usually unfold over time rather than all at once. A person may read a chapter like this today, file or delay months from now, and then have to revisit the same ideas after a work change, a health event, a market decline, a Medicare transition, or the loss of a spouse. Good education should still be useful when life moves. That is one reason simple frameworks tend to serve people better than one-time slogans.

It is also worth noticing how often confidence grows when people stop asking for the perfect universal answer and start asking for the right answer for this season of life. The same household may need one strategy at sixty-two, a different strategy at sixty-six, and a different review again after Medicare begins or after one spouse dies. The rules matter, but the calendar of real life matters too. A thoughtful retirement review respects that timing instead of pretending every decision can be made once and ignored forever.

One final point is easy to underestimate: retirement decisions are rarely judged by math alone. They are lived out in monthly routines, family conversations, health changes, and the emotional experience of aging. A strategy that is technically impressive but constantly creates worry may not be the strongest strategy for that household. On the other hand, a strategy that supports steadier habits and clearer expectations may prove more durable over time. That is why practical fit belongs in the conversation right alongside rules and projections.

In that sense, planning around taxes, medicare, and hidden costs is not only about information. It is also about alignment. The numbers matter. The rules matter. But the household's values matter too. Some people care deeply about future survivor protection. Some care most about present cash-flow relief. Some want to preserve flexibility because life has already taught them plans can change. A well-guided review makes room for those priorities without letting the conversation drift into guesswork.

That is why the most valuable outcome from this chapter is not memorizing one more rule. The real value is becoming better prepared for a personal review. When you can describe what concerns you, what facts you have, and what tradeoffs matter most, the next conversation becomes more productive. Clarity grows when the discussion moves from a generic topic to your actual retirement picture.

This is one of the most practical chapters because spendable income matters more than the gross benefit. Taxes and Medicare premiums can change the amount a household truly has available.

For 2026 planning, IRMAA and Social Security taxation should be discussed in plain language. The goal is not to make the reader a tax expert, but to keep them from being blindsided.

A Retiree Who Focused Only on the Gross Benefit

Donna was pleased to start Social Security and saw it as a relief after years of working. Later, she realized that her IRA withdrawals, pension income, and Medicare premiums made the net result feel smaller than expected.

Nothing unusual had happened. She simply had not looked at the pieces together. The benefit amount was real, but the spendable amount was shaped by more than the Social Security statement alone.

Once she understood that, her planning conversation improved. Instead of asking only how much Social Security she would receive, she began asking how much income she was likely to keep after other moving parts were considered.

The IRMAA Surprise

Gary and Theresa had a year with larger-than-normal income because of retirement account moves and other taxable events. Later, their Medicare premiums increased due to income-based adjustments.

They did not connect those premium changes to broader income planning until after the fact. Their Social Security decision was not the sole cause, but it was part of a larger picture that had not been coordinated carefully.

This kind of surprise is one reason retirement income planning, Medicare planning, and Social Security planning work better when they are discussed together rather than in separate silos.

What People Often Think

People often think Social Security is either taxed or not taxed, as if there are only two simple categories. The reality is more layered.

They also often think Medicare premiums are fixed and unrelated to broader income planning. In many households, that assumption turns out to be costly.

Another common belief is that if an online calculator shows a monthly estimate, that number is close enough for planning. The estimate is helpful, but it is not a net-income plan.

What Actually Happens

What actually happens is that retirement income sources stack on top of each other. Social Security, pensions, IRA distributions, Roth decisions, part-time work, and investment income can change both tax exposure and Medicare premium outcomes.

What actually happens is that some households benefit from coordinating the sequence and size of withdrawals before and after claiming. Even simple adjustments can improve clarity.

What actually happens is that the strongest plans pay attention to spendable income, not just promised income. That mindset often leads to better retirement conversations.

Where People Get Stuck

People get stuck because taxes feel technical and Medicare premiums feel separate, so they postpone the discussion.

They also get stuck when a spouse handles one topic and the other spouse handles another. The household may have pieces of the answer but not a shared picture.

Another place people get stuck is when they are embarrassed by complexity. They may think they should already understand how benefits are taxed or how IRMAA works. In reality, these are some of the most common retirement blind spots.

What We Typically Review Together

Tax filing status and the likely mix of taxable and non-taxable retirement income sources.

Whether IRA withdrawals, pensions, or work income could change the taxation of benefits.

Current or expected Medicare enrollment and whether IRMAA may become a concern.

The difference between gross Social Security income and spendable monthly income.

Whether broader retirement income planning can smooth out surprises over time.

Social Security is connected to taxes, Medicare, and retirement income. That connection is worth repeating because it is where many otherwise thoughtful retirees get tripped up. Timing is personal. Online tools are starting points, not final answers. General advice is not the same as personal guidance. Claiming decisions can affect long-term income and survivor planning in ways that are easy to miss when the conversation stays too narrow.

Chapter Summary

Taxes and Medicare can quietly reshape what Social Security means in real life. That is why planning around the gross estimate alone is rarely enough.

When people understand how income, taxes, and Medicare interact, they usually make calmer and more informed decisions.

If you would like help reviewing how Social Security fits into your broader retirement picture, you can schedule a personalized review at:

https://host.safemsngr.com/widget/bookings/psgss

Medicare education resources are also available at:

https://learnmedicare.org/home

Chapter 7: Spousal Benefits

This chapter matters because many married couples assume two work histories automatically produce two independent decisions. That is not always how the real planning conversation unfolds.

Spousal rules can create opportunities, but they can also create confusion when couples try to self-calculate everything from memory, internet charts, or stories from friends.

Simple Explanation

In simple terms, a spouse may be eligible for a benefit based on the other spouse's work record if certain rules are met. The amount and timing depend on several factors, including age, the worker's filing status, and the spouse's own benefit record.

A common simplified reference point is that a spouse at full retirement age may receive up to one-half of the worker's primary insurance amount, not one-half of a delayed age 70 amount. But that statement is only the start of the conversation. Filing before full retirement age can reduce the spousal amount, and a spouse's own work record can affect what is actually paid.

This is one area where small misunderstandings can create big confidence problems. People hear one fact and assume they understand the whole rule. Then real-world details start to complicate the picture.

For that reason, spousal planning should feel educational but not overly do-it-yourself. Couples should understand the broad framework, yet still review their own records carefully before assuming how much one spouse will receive or when that amount can begin.

Coordination Note

A spouse's benefit can be up to one-half of the worker's full-retirement-age amount, but that does not mean a spouse simply receives half of whatever the other spouse is currently collecting.

Age at filing, the worker's status, and the spouse's own retirement benefit all matter. In many households, Social Security first looks at the spouse's own benefit and then pays the higher eligible amount rather than adding the payment amounts together. That is one reason couples are usually better served by a coordinated review than by trying to estimate the result from one chart.

Planning Perspective

One reason spousal benefits deserves more space than a quick article or a short seminar comment is that the subject does not stay inside its own lane for very long. A person may begin by asking a straightforward question, then discover that the answer depends on work plans, marital status, spending needs, tax exposure, health concerns, or survivor priorities. That is why a chapter like this is not meant to overwhelm you with detail. It is meant to slow the conversation down enough for the important tradeoffs to become visible.

In real households, this topic usually shows up beside other retirement questions rather than by itself. Someone may be thinking about Both spouses' estimated benefits and filing ages, while also trying to sort out whether one spouse has a significantly higher work record. Another household may be focused on how household income needs change if one spouse retires sooner than the other and only later realize that Social Security timing is part of the same story. When pieces arrive in that order, the decision can feel more confusing than it really is. Often what is missing is not intelligence. It is simply a calm way to organize the moving parts.

This is also where broad guidance reaches its limit. A chart can teach. A rule of thumb can simplify. An online estimate can point you in the right direction. None of those tools can fully measure what retirement feels like inside one specific household. They do not know how cautious you are, how steady your income needs will be, how one spouse feels compared with the other, or how much flexibility you need if life changes. That is why education is helpful and still not the same thing as personal guidance.

Readers are often relieved when they realize they do not have to solve every part of this alone. You do not need to become your own Social Security office, tax preparer, Medicare analyst, and retirement-income engineer all at once. What you do need is enough understanding to recognize when a decision deserves a wider review. That is a very different goal from trying to self-manage every technical issue from scratch.

A thoughtful review usually changes the tone of the conversation. Instead of asking only, 'What is the biggest number?' people begin asking more useful questions. Which choice protects the household better over time? Which choice fits the way retirement income will actually be used? Which choice respects taxes, Medicare, and survivor concerns instead of discovering them later? Those are not dramatic questions. They are mature planning questions, and they often lead to steadier decisions.

Another reason to revisit this topic carefully is that retirement decisions usually unfold over time rather than all at once. A person may read a chapter like this today, file or delay months from now, and then have to revisit the same ideas after a work change, a health event, a market decline, a Medicare transition, or the loss of a spouse. Good education should still be useful when life moves. That is one reason simple frameworks tend to serve people better than one-time slogans.

It is also worth noticing how often confidence grows when people stop asking for the perfect universal answer and start asking for the right answer for this season of life. The same household may need one strategy at sixty-two, a different strategy at sixty-six, and a different review again after Medicare begins or after one spouse dies. The rules matter, but the calendar of real life matters too. A thoughtful retirement review respects that timing instead of pretending every decision can be made once and ignored forever.

One final point is easy to underestimate: retirement decisions are rarely judged by math alone. They are lived out in monthly routines, family conversations, health changes, and the emotional

experience of aging. A strategy that is technically impressive but constantly creates worry may not be the strongest strategy for that household. On the other hand, a strategy that supports steadier habits and clearer expectations may prove more durable over time. That is why practical fit belongs in the conversation right alongside rules and projections.

In that sense, planning around spousal benefits is not only about information. It is also about alignment. The numbers matter. The rules matter. But the household's values matter too. Some people care deeply about future survivor protection. Some care most about present cash-flow relief. Some want to preserve flexibility because life has already taught them plans can change. A well-guided review makes room for those priorities without letting the conversation drift into guesswork.

That is why the most valuable outcome from this chapter is not memorizing one more rule. The real value is becoming better prepared for a personal review. When you can describe what concerns you, what facts you have, and what tradeoffs matter most, the next conversation becomes more productive. Clarity grows when the discussion moves from a generic topic to your actual retirement picture.

Spousal benefits are often misunderstood because households think in terms of two checks, while the rules look at eligibility, timing, and coordination.

Couples are usually better served by reviewing both records together. One spouse's decision can affect the other spouse's income now and the survivor's income later.

One Strong Earner and One Lower Earner

Anthony and Maria expected Maria's benefit to be based mainly on Anthony's work history because she spent many years working part-time while raising children.

The broad concept was true, but the details still mattered. Maria had her own earnings record, Anthony's filing age affected the discussion, and their overall retirement timing changed how soon either benefit would begin. Their strategy could not be reduced to one sentence about getting 'half of his benefit.'

Once they reviewed the rules in a more personal way, the conversation became clearer and far less stressful.

Two Spouses With Different Retirement Timelines

Leon wanted to keep working until 70, while Cynthia was ready to retire sooner. They assumed their Social Security decisions could simply be made separately.

That assumption created confusion because the couple needed to think about spousal coordination, household cash flow, and the possibility that one spouse would rely more heavily on the other's record later. Their retirement dates were different, but their planning still overlapped.

This is why spousal benefit conversations work best when the household is reviewed together rather than as two unrelated claim forms.

What People Often Think

People often think a spouse automatically gets half of whatever the other spouse receives. That is one of the most common misunderstandings.

Others think spousal benefits are easy to estimate because the rules sound simple in conversation. The details are usually more layered than they first appear.

Another common belief is that if both spouses worked, then spousal planning does not matter. In many households, it still matters a great deal.

What Actually Happens

What actually happens is that spousal benefits depend on several moving parts at once. Filing ages, work records, eligibility timing, and household income needs all matter.

What actually happens is that the higher earner's choice may influence more than one person. Even when each spouse has an earnings record, the coordination still deserves attention.

What actually happens is that couples who slow down and review the broader picture tend to make better decisions than couples who try to simplify the rules down to one sentence.

Where People Get Stuck

People get stuck because spousal rules sound familiar but not fully clear. They know enough to worry that there is more to the story.

They also get stuck when one spouse is more interested in the details than the other. That can leave part of the household carrying all of the decision pressure.

Another place couples struggle is in assuming that a general article applies cleanly to them, even when work histories, age gaps, or retirement timing differ from the example.

What We Typically Review Together

Both spouses' estimated benefits and filing ages.

Whether one spouse has a significantly higher work record.

How household income needs change if one spouse retires sooner than the other.

How taxes, Medicare timing, and other income sources affect the couple's combined strategy.

Whether the claiming approach also supports future survivor planning.

Social Security is connected to taxes, Medicare, and retirement income. That connection is worth repeating because it is where many otherwise thoughtful retirees get tripped up. Timing is personal. Online tools are starting points, not final answers. General advice is not the same as personal guidance. Claiming decisions can affect long-term income and survivor planning in ways that are easy to miss when the conversation stays too narrow.

Chapter Summary

Spousal benefits can be valuable, but they are rarely well served by quick assumptions. Even simple-looking rules need household context.

For couples, Social Security is often more connected than it first appears.

Spousal planning naturally leads to an even more important protection question: what happens after the first death in the household? The next chapter explains survivor benefits and why they deserve more attention than many couples initially give them.

Chapter 8: Survivor Benefits

This chapter matters because many couples plan most actively for the years when both spouses are alive, yet one of the most financially vulnerable periods in retirement can begin after the first spouse dies.

Survivor planning is not only a legal or emotional issue. It is an income issue. Social Security plays an important role in that conversation.

Simple Explanation

When one spouse dies, the surviving spouse may be eligible for survivor benefits, subject to Social Security rules. In many cases, the surviving spouse keeps the larger of the two benefit amounts rather than receiving both full checks. That means the couple can move from two checks down to one larger check.

This is why the higher earner's claiming decision matters so much in married-couple planning. A larger retirement benefit created by delaying can later become a larger survivor benefit. For some households, that is one of the strongest arguments for taking the survivor perspective seriously.

At the same time, survivor planning should not be reduced to Social Security alone. After the first death, household income may go down while certain expenses remain, and some expenses may rise. Tax filing status may change. The surviving spouse may also face new decisions around housing, health care, or long-term care.

That broader reality creates a natural bridge into retirement income planning, safe money conversations, annuity education, protection planning, and legacy planning. Those topics are not separate from survivor concerns. They are often part of the same household protection discussion.

Survivor Benefit Clarification

When one spouse dies, the surviving spouse may be eligible for a survivor benefit based on the deceased spouse's record. In many situations, that does not mean two full Social Security checks continue.

It usually means the surviving spouse receives the payment that is best for them rather than both amounts together. In some cases, the person may also start with one type of benefit and switch later, which is another reason survivor planning deserves a personal review instead of a quick assumption.

Planning Perspective

One reason survivor benefits deserves more space than a quick article or a short seminar comment is that the subject does not stay inside its own lane for very long. A person may begin by asking a straightforward question, then discover that the answer depends on work plans, marital status, spending needs, tax exposure, health concerns, or survivor priorities. That is why a chapter like this is not meant to overwhelm you with detail. It is meant to slow the conversation down enough for the important tradeoffs to become visible.

In real households, this topic usually shows up beside other retirement questions rather than by itself. Someone may be thinking about Which spouse has the higher benefit and how that affects future survivor income, while also trying to sort out whether delaying the higher earner's benefit fits the household's present cash flow. Another household may be focused on how expenses may change after the first death and which costs are likely to remain and only later realize that Social Security timing is part of the same story. When pieces arrive in that order, the decision can feel more confusing than it really is. Often what is missing is not intelligence. It is simply a calm way to organize the moving parts.

This is also where broad guidance reaches its limit. A chart can teach. A rule of thumb can simplify. An online estimate can point you in the right direction. None of those tools can fully measure what retirement feels like inside one specific household. They do not know how cautious you are, how steady your income needs will be, how one spouse feels compared with the other, or how much flexibility you need if life changes. That is why education is helpful and still not the same thing as personal guidance.

Readers are often relieved when they realize they do not have to solve every part of this alone. You do not need to become your own Social Security office, tax preparer, Medicare analyst, and retirement-income engineer all at once. What you do need is enough understanding to recognize when a decision deserves a wider review. That is a very different goal from trying to self-manage every technical issue from scratch.

A thoughtful review usually changes the tone of the conversation. Instead of asking only, 'What is the biggest number?' people begin asking more useful questions. Which choice protects the household better over time? Which choice fits the way retirement income will actually be used? Which choice respects taxes, Medicare, and survivor concerns instead of discovering them later? Those are not dramatic questions. They are mature planning questions, and they often lead to steadier decisions.

Another reason to revisit this topic carefully is that retirement decisions usually unfold over time rather than all at once. A person may read a chapter like this today, file or delay months from now, and then have to revisit the same ideas after a work change, a health event, a market decline, a Medicare transition, or the loss of a spouse. Good education should still be useful when life moves. That is one reason simple frameworks tend to serve people better than one-time slogans.

It is also worth noticing how often confidence grows when people stop asking for the perfect universal answer and start asking for the right answer for this season of life. The same household may need one strategy at sixty-two, a different strategy at sixty-six, and a different review again after Medicare begins or after one spouse dies. The rules matter, but the calendar of real life matters too. A thoughtful retirement review respects that timing instead of pretending every decision can be made once and ignored forever.

One final point is easy to underestimate: retirement decisions are rarely judged by math alone. They are lived out in monthly routines, family conversations, health changes, and the emotional experience of aging. A strategy that is technically impressive but constantly creates worry may not be the strongest strategy for that household. On the other hand, a strategy that supports steadier habits and clearer expectations may prove more durable over time. That is why practical fit belongs in the conversation right alongside rules and projections.

In that sense, planning around survivor benefits is not only about information. It is also about alignment. The numbers matter. The rules matter. But the household's values matter too. Some people care deeply about future survivor protection. Some care most about present cash-flow relief. Some want to preserve flexibility because life has already taught them plans can change. A well-guided review makes room for those priorities without letting the conversation drift into guesswork.

That is why the most valuable outcome from this chapter is not memorizing one more rule. The real value is becoming better prepared for a personal review. When you can describe what concerns you, what facts you have, and what tradeoffs matter most, the next conversation becomes more productive. Clarity grows when the discussion moves from a generic topic to your actual retirement picture.

Survivor planning is not just a technical rule. It is a household protection issue, especially when one spouse has a much larger earnings record.

A decision that looks fine while both spouses are alive may feel very different after one spouse dies. That is why survivor income deserves attention before the household is under stress.

The Higher Earner's Delay as Survivor Protection

Martin was tempted to claim as soon as he retired at 63. His wife, JoAnn, had a smaller earnings record and was likely to live on the larger of the two benefits if he died first.

When the conversation was framed only around Martin's current needs, early claiming seemed comfortable. When the conversation widened to survivor income, the tradeoff looked different. Delaying part of the plan could strengthen the check that might later matter most to JoAnn.

The decision still had to fit their cash flow and savings, but the survivor lens helped them see a bigger purpose behind the timing choice.

A Surviving Spouse Learning Too Much Too Late

After her husband died, Cheryl discovered that going from two benefits to one changed the household more than she had expected. Utility bills, housing costs, and health-related expenses did not fall in proportion to the lost income.

Her Social Security rules were not wrong. They were simply not the full story. What she needed most was a coordinated understanding of survivor income, expenses, taxes, and available assets.

That is why survivor planning is best handled before a crisis rather than after one.

What People Often Think

People often think survivor planning can wait because it feels uncomfortable or far away.

Others think if both spouses receive Social Security, the surviving spouse will just continue with roughly the same household income. That is rarely the case.

Another common belief is that survivor planning belongs only in estate planning conversations. In reality, it is deeply connected to income planning.

What Actually Happens

What actually happens is that the surviving spouse may face a meaningful income shift. Even when one larger Social Security benefit remains, the total household income can drop substantially.

What actually happens is that the higher earner's claiming decision can affect the strength of that future survivor benefit. That makes timing personal not only for today's retiree, but for tomorrow's surviving spouse.

What actually happens is that survivor planning often leads naturally into conversations about guaranteed income, safe money, annuity education, protection planning, and how to reduce the financial strain of a one-income household later in life.

Where People Get Stuck

People get stuck because the topic is emotionally difficult. Talking about one spouse outliving the other can feel heavy even when it is necessary.

They also get stuck when they focus only on assets and not on income structure. A retirement account balance may look reassuring, but the practical question is often how the surviving spouse will live month to month.

Another place households struggle is in assuming the survivor benefit rules will be obvious when the time comes. It is better to become familiar with the broad picture ahead of time.

What We Typically Review Together

Which spouse has the higher benefit and how that affects future survivor income.

Whether delaying the higher earner's benefit fits the household's present cash flow.

How expenses may change after the first death and which costs are likely to remain.

What other income sources, safe money strategies, or annuity-based income options may support the surviving spouse.

Whether life insurance, long-term care planning, and legacy goals should also be part of the review.

Social Security is connected to taxes, Medicare, and retirement income. That connection is worth repeating because it is where many otherwise thoughtful retirees get tripped up. Timing is personal. Online tools are starting points, not final answers. General advice is not the same as personal guidance. Claiming decisions can affect long-term income and survivor planning in ways that are easy to miss when the conversation stays too narrow.

Chapter Summary

Survivor benefits are not a side topic. For many couples, they are one of the most important reasons to treat Social Security timing carefully.

When survivor income is reviewed alongside the broader retirement picture, households often make steadier decisions.

Once survivor planning is in view, it becomes easier to understand why special situations can change the conversation so much. The next chapter looks at divorce, remarriage, government pension issues, disability, and other circumstances that deserve careful handling.

Chapter 9: Divorce, Remarriage, and Special Situations

This chapter matters because many people assume Social Security rules apply the same way to everyone until they discover that divorce, remarriage, pensions, disability, or other life events can materially change the picture.

Special situations do not mean impossible situations. They simply mean the review needs to be more careful.

Simple Explanation

Divorced spouse benefits may be available if certain conditions are met, including the length of the prior marriage and age-related rules. For many readers, the most important takeaway is not to self-diagnose eligibility based on one article or one conversation. The rules can be technical, and details matter.

Remarriage can also affect benefit options depending on the type of benefit involved and the timing of the remarriage. People are often surprised to learn that a second marriage can change assumptions they have carried for years.

Government pension issues deserve special mention. The Social Security Fairness Act, signed on January 5, 2025, ended the Windfall Elimination Provision and Government Pension Offset. As a result, WEP and GPO no longer reduce benefits for many affected individuals. Even so, administrative implementation and individual records still need to be verified, especially where prior estimates or expectations were shaped under the old rules.

Disability and other special circumstances can also affect planning decisions. Some households are not deciding between a clean retirement path at all. They are navigating health changes, reduced work ability, or family care responsibilities at the same time. That is another reason general advice only goes so far.

Divorce and Remarriage Basics

Divorced spouse benefits and survivor benefits often depend on details such as the length of the marriage, current marital status, and the timing of remarriage. For example, the 10-year marriage rule is an important starting point in many divorced-spouse conversations.

Survivor benefit eligibility can also be affected by remarriage timing. Because these rules are detail-sensitive, this chapter should be treated as a signal to review the facts carefully rather than as a substitute for personal guidance.

Current Rule Note: WEP and GPO

Government pension issues deserve special attention. The Social Security Fairness Act was signed on January 5, 2025, and December 2023 was the last month that WEP and GPO applied. In other words, those provisions no longer apply to benefits payable for January 2024 and later.

Even so, benefit records, retroactive adjustments, and current payment details should still be verified before anyone assumes the final result. Public-sector employment, prior pension rules, and old benefit estimates can create confusion if they are not reviewed against current records.

Planning Perspective

One reason divorce, remarriage, and special situations deserves more space than a quick article or a short seminar comment is that the subject does not stay inside its own lane for very long. A person may begin by asking a straightforward question, then discover that the answer depends on work plans, marital status, spending needs, tax exposure, health concerns, or survivor priorities. That is why a chapter like this is not meant to overwhelm you with detail. It is meant to slow the conversation down enough for the important tradeoffs to become visible.

In real households, this topic usually shows up beside other retirement questions rather than by itself. Someone may be thinking about Prior marriages, current marital status, and whether remarriage timing affects planning assumptions, while also trying to sort out Government pension history and whether prior WEP or GPO expectations should be revisited under the Social Security Fairness Act. Another household may be focused on Whether disability, health events, or caregiving demands are changing work and retirement plans and only later realize that Social Security timing is part of the same story. When pieces arrive in that order, the decision can feel more confusing than it really is. Often what is missing is not intelligence. It is simply a calm way to organize the moving parts.

This is also where broad guidance reaches its limit. A chart can teach. A rule of thumb can simplify. An online estimate can point you in the right direction. None of those tools can fully measure what retirement feels like inside one specific household. They do not know how cautious you are, how steady your income needs will be, how one spouse feels compared with the other, or how much flexibility you need if life changes. That is why education is helpful and still not the same thing as personal guidance.

Readers are often relieved when they realize they do not have to solve every part of this alone. You do not need to become your own Social Security office, tax preparer, Medicare analyst, and retirement-income engineer all at once. What you do need is enough understanding to recognize when a decision deserves a wider review. That is a very different goal from trying to self-manage every technical issue from scratch.

A thoughtful review usually changes the tone of the conversation. Instead of asking only, 'What is the biggest number?' people begin asking more useful questions. Which choice protects the household better over time? Which choice fits the way retirement income will actually be used? Which choice respects taxes, Medicare, and survivor concerns instead of discovering them later? Those are not dramatic questions. They are mature planning questions, and they often lead to steadier decisions.

Another reason to revisit this topic carefully is that retirement decisions usually unfold over time rather than all at once. A person may read a chapter like this today, file or delay months from now, and then have to revisit the same ideas after a work change, a health event, a market decline, a Medicare transition, or the loss of a spouse. Good education should still be useful when life moves. That is one reason simple frameworks tend to serve people better than one-time slogans.

It is also worth noticing how often confidence grows when people stop asking for the perfect universal answer and start asking for the right answer for this season of life. The same household may need one strategy at sixty-two, a different strategy at sixty-six, and a different review again after Medicare begins or after one spouse dies. The rules matter, but the calendar of real life matters too. A thoughtful retirement review respects that timing instead of pretending every decision can be made once and ignored forever.

One final point is easy to underestimate: retirement decisions are rarely judged by math alone. They are lived out in monthly routines, family conversations, health changes, and the emotional experience of aging. A strategy that is technically impressive but constantly creates worry may not be the strongest strategy for that household. On the other hand, a strategy that supports steadier habits and clearer expectations may prove more durable over time. That is why practical fit belongs in the conversation right alongside rules and projections.

In that sense, planning around divorce, remarriage, and special situations is not only about information. It is also about alignment. The numbers matter. The rules matter. But the household's values matter too. Some people care deeply about future survivor protection. Some care most about present cash-flow relief. Some want to preserve flexibility because life has already taught them plans can change. A well-guided review makes room for those priorities without letting the conversation drift into guesswork.

That is why the most valuable outcome from this chapter is not memorizing one more rule. The real value is becoming better prepared for a personal review. When you can describe what concerns you, what facts you have, and what tradeoffs matter most, the next conversation becomes more productive. Clarity grows when the discussion moves from a generic topic to your actual retirement picture.

Special situations are where assumptions become especially risky. Divorce, remarriage, public-sector pensions, and disability-related questions can change the analysis quickly.

This chapter should help readers recognize when a situation deserves closer review rather than trying to force the facts into a basic retirement example.

A Divorced Spouse With Old Assumptions

Linda had been divorced for years and assumed the topic no longer mattered to her Social Security decisions. She had heard pieces of information over time but never knew which rules actually applied.

When she finally reviewed the situation more carefully, she realized that some of her long-held assumptions were incomplete. The goal was not to memorize every technical rule. The goal was to understand which questions belonged in her personal review.

That alone reduced a lot of uncertainty. She moved from vague worry to informed follow-up.

A Public-Sector Retiree Rechecking Old Expectations

Robert had spent years hearing that WEP or GPO would reduce what he could expect because part of his career involved a pension from work not covered by Social Security.

After the Social Security Fairness Act changed the landscape, he still needed to verify how the new law affected his own record and timing. Broad headlines were encouraging, but personal confirmation still mattered.

His situation was a good reminder that even favorable rule changes should be reviewed carefully before someone assumes the final result.

What People Often Think

People often think special situations are rare and therefore probably do not apply to them. In practice, many households have at least one complicating factor.

They also often think a major headline settles the issue. Legal changes are important, but personal records and implementation details still matter.

Another common belief is that a divorced spouse or public-sector retiree should be able to figure everything out from charts alone. That expectation usually creates more confusion than clarity.

What Actually Happens

What actually happens is that special situations amplify the value of a personal review. Life events change the questions that need to be asked.

What actually happens is that divorce, remarriage, pension history, and disability considerations can reshape timelines, expectations, and available options.

What actually happens is that readers benefit most when they understand the broad concepts and then verify their own facts rather than relying on assumptions that may be outdated or incomplete.

Where People Get Stuck

People get stuck because they worry they are asking the wrong question or revealing that they do not understand the rules.

They also get stuck when old advice lingers in their memory long after rules or family circumstances have changed.

Another place people stall is in thinking they need a final answer before they begin the conversation. In reality, the conversation is often what uncovers the right question.

What We Typically Review Together

Prior marriages, current marital status, and whether remarriage timing affects planning assumptions.

Government pension history and whether prior WEP or GPO expectations should be revisited under the Social Security Fairness Act.

Whether disability, health events, or caregiving demands are changing work and retirement plans.

What personal records or statements need to be confirmed before a claiming decision is made.

Whether taxes, Medicare, and survivor planning are still aligned under the revised fact pattern.

Social Security is connected to taxes, Medicare, and retirement income. That connection is worth repeating because it is where many otherwise thoughtful retirees get tripped up. Timing is personal. Online tools are starting points, not final answers. General advice is not the same as personal guidance. Claiming decisions can affect long-term income and survivor planning in ways that are easy to miss when the conversation stays too narrow.

Chapter Summary

Special situations do not mean the rules are impossible, but they do mean the shortcuts are less reliable.

When divorce, remarriage, pension history, or disability enters the conversation, a thoughtful review becomes even more valuable.

By now it is easier to see that Social Security is one component of a much bigger plan. The next chapter steps back and shows how benefits coordinate with pensions, retirement accounts, withdrawals, taxes, Medicare, and monthly cash flow.

Chapter 10: Coordinating Social Security with Retirement Income

This chapter matters because Social Security rarely works best as a standalone decision. It almost always needs to be coordinated with the other income sources that will support retirement.

When people see the claiming decision as part of a cash-flow plan rather than an isolated government benefit, the conversation usually becomes clearer and more practical.

Simple Explanation

Most retirees draw income from more than one place. Social Security may be combined with pensions, retirement accounts, brokerage assets, part-time work, rental income, or business income. The order and timing of those income sources can affect confidence, taxes, Medicare, and lifestyle flexibility.

For example, some households use savings as a bridge so they can delay Social Security and lock in a larger future benefit. Others use Social Security earlier to reduce pressure on investment accounts, especially when market volatility or spending concerns make large withdrawals uncomfortable.

There is no universal rule that one income source should always be used first. What matters is how the pieces fit together. A household with a strong pension may think about timing differently than a household relying heavily on IRAs. A single retiree may think differently than a married couple with survivor concerns.

This coordination is also where tax planning often becomes more meaningful. The way withdrawals are sequenced may change the taxability of benefits, the risk of higher Medicare premiums, and the overall stability of the retirement income stream.

Planning Perspective

One reason coordinating social security with retirement income deserves more space than a quick article or a short seminar comment is that the subject does not stay inside its own lane for very long. A person may begin by asking a straightforward question, then discover that the answer depends on work plans, marital status, spending needs, tax exposure, health concerns, or survivor priorities. That is why a chapter like this is not meant to overwhelm you with detail. It is meant to slow the conversation down enough for the important tradeoffs to become visible.

In real households, this topic usually shows up beside other retirement questions rather than by itself. Someone may be thinking about Expected Social Security income alongside pensions, savings, retirement accounts, and any ongoing work, while also trying to sort out whether using assets before claiming later would strengthen or strain the long-term plan. Another household may be focused on how the sequence of withdrawals may affect taxes and Medicare premiums and only later realize that Social Security timing is part of the same story. When pieces arrive in that order, the decision can feel more confusing than it really is. Often what is missing is not intelligence. It is simply a calm way to organize the moving parts.

This is also where broad guidance reaches its limit. A chart can teach. A rule of thumb can simplify. An online estimate can point you in the right direction. None of those tools can fully measure what retirement feels like inside one specific household. They do not know how cautious you are, how steady your income needs will be, how one spouse feels compared with the other, or how much flexibility you need if life changes. That is why education is helpful and still not the same thing as personal guidance.

Readers are often relieved when they realize they do not have to solve every part of this alone. You do not need to become your own Social Security office, tax preparer, Medicare analyst, and retirement-income engineer all at once. What you do need is enough understanding to recognize when a decision deserves a wider review. That is a very different goal from trying to self-manage every technical issue from scratch.

A thoughtful review usually changes the tone of the conversation. Instead of asking only, 'What is the biggest number?' people begin asking more useful questions. Which choice protects the household better over time? Which choice fits the way retirement income will actually be used? Which choice respects taxes, Medicare, and survivor concerns instead of discovering them later? Those are not dramatic questions. They are mature planning questions, and they often lead to steadier decisions.

Another reason to revisit this topic carefully is that retirement decisions usually unfold over time rather than all at once. A person may read a chapter like this today, file or delay months from now, and then have to revisit the same ideas after a work change, a health event, a market decline, a Medicare transition, or the loss of a spouse. Good education should still be useful when life moves. That is one reason simple frameworks tend to serve people better than one-time slogans.

It is also worth noticing how often confidence grows when people stop asking for the perfect universal answer and start asking for the right answer for this season of life. The same household may need one strategy at sixty-two, a different strategy at sixty-six, and a different review again after Medicare begins or after one spouse dies. The rules matter, but the calendar of real life matters too. A thoughtful retirement review respects that timing instead of pretending every decision can be made once and ignored forever.

One final point is easy to underestimate: retirement decisions are rarely judged by math alone. They are lived out in monthly routines, family conversations, health changes, and the emotional experience of aging. A strategy that is technically impressive but constantly creates worry may not be the strongest strategy for that household. On the other hand, a strategy that supports steadier habits and clearer expectations may prove more durable over time. That is why practical fit belongs in the conversation right alongside rules and projections.

In that sense, planning around coordinating social security with retirement income is not only about information. It is also about alignment. The numbers matter. The rules matter. But the household's values matter too. Some people care deeply about future survivor protection. Some care most about present cash-flow relief. Some want to preserve flexibility because life has already taught them plans can change. A well-guided review makes room for those priorities without letting the conversation drift into guesswork.

That is why the most valuable outcome from this chapter is not memorizing one more rule. The real value is becoming better prepared for a personal review. When you can describe what concerns you, what facts you have, and what tradeoffs matter most, the next conversation becomes more productive. Clarity grows when the discussion moves from a generic topic to your actual retirement picture.

Social Security is one income source, not the entire income plan. The order in which income is used can affect taxes, Medicare costs, savings longevity, and peace of mind.

The planning question becomes: what income should be used, when, and for what purpose? That is a broader conversation than simply choosing a Social Security start date.

Using Savings as a Delayed-Claim Bridge

Elaine and Todd had enough savings to cover a few years of retirement spending before Social Security began. Their question was whether doing so would actually improve the long-term plan or simply feel like spending down assets for no reason.

Once the household cash-flow plan was modeled in a practical way, they could compare the tradeoff between near-term withdrawals and stronger guaranteed income later. The answer was not automatic, but the framework was far better than guessing.

The process helped them see that Social Security timing and portfolio withdrawals were connected decisions, not separate ones.

Claiming Earlier to Reduce Portfolio Stress

Neil had no pension and was uncomfortable with the idea of drawing too heavily from investments during an uncertain market stretch. Although waiting would have increased his future Social Security amount, claiming earlier brought emotional and financial relief to the income plan he could actually stick with.

That did not make early claiming universally superior. It made it appropriate for a household that valued lower portfolio pressure and greater present cash-flow certainty.

Retirement plans have to be livable, not merely theoretical.

What People Often Think

People often think Social Security should be decided first and the rest of the income plan handled later.

Others think retirement accounts are just a separate bucket that can be tapped as needed, without affecting the Social Security conversation. In practice, the buckets interact.

Another common belief is that if an online calculator shows a favorable claiming age, the broader cash-flow plan will naturally fall into place. It usually does not work that way.

What Actually Happens

What actually happens is that retirement income planning becomes stronger when income sources are coordinated rather than layered on haphazardly.

What actually happens is that Social Security can either reduce or increase pressure on other assets depending on the timing choice and the household's goals.

What actually happens is that the best strategy often balances guaranteed income, liquidity, tax awareness, and flexibility instead of maximizing one number in isolation.

Where People Get Stuck

People get stuck because they have accounts, statements, and estimates, but not an organized income story.

They also get stuck when they fear spending down savings even if doing so might support a stronger long-term income structure.

Another place households stall is in not knowing which professional conversation comes first: Social Security, taxes, Medicare, investments, or insurance. The truth is that the best reviews often connect those conversations rather than forcing them apart.

What We Typically Review Together

Expected Social Security income alongside pensions, savings, retirement accounts, and any ongoing work.

Whether using assets before claiming later would strengthen or strain the long-term plan.

How the sequence of withdrawals may affect taxes and Medicare premiums.

What level of guaranteed income the household wants versus market-dependent income.

Whether survivor planning changes the value of delaying one spouse's benefit.

Social Security is connected to taxes, Medicare, and retirement income. That connection is worth repeating because it is where many otherwise thoughtful retirees get tripped up. Timing is personal. Online tools are starting points, not final answers. General advice is not the same as personal guidance. Claiming decisions can affect long-term income and survivor planning in ways that are easy to miss when the conversation stays too narrow.

Chapter Summary

Social Security makes more sense when viewed as part of the retirement income system rather than as a separate decision.

Coordinating benefits with savings, pensions, withdrawals, taxes, and Medicare often leads to a more stable plan.

That coordination naturally raises a broader retirement planning question: if there may be an income gap or a need for more predictable income, what tools deserve consideration? The next chapter introduces safe money strategies and annuity education in a balanced way.

Chapter 11: Safe Money, Annuities, and Income Gaps

This chapter matters because Social Security does not have to carry the full burden of retirement income planning by itself. Many households need to think about where additional stability may come from.

That is where safe money conversations sometimes enter the picture. Not every retiree needs the same tools, but many benefit from understanding how more predictable income strategies may fit alongside Social Security.

Simple Explanation

The phrase safe money can mean different things in different conversations, but it generally refers to assets or strategies intended to prioritize preservation, predictability, or reduced market exposure compared with more volatile growth-oriented investments. The appropriate role, if any, depends on the household.

Annuities are one topic that often appears in these conversations. They are not one single product and should not be treated as a simple yes-or-no category. Some annuities are discussed because they may help create more predictable income. Others are evaluated for principal protection features, accumulation goals, or long-term planning considerations.

The right question is not whether annuities are universally good or universally bad. The right question is whether a particular strategy solves a real planning problem. For some retirees, the problem is an income gap between retirement and delayed Social Security. For others, the problem is concern about market volatility, survivor income, or running out of predictable cash flow later in life.

This conversation should stay educational and balanced. Products are not a substitute for planning. A household should understand what role a tool is intended to play, what tradeoffs come with it, and how it fits with Social Security, Medicare, taxes, liquidity needs, and legacy goals.

As always, guarantees associated with annuities or life insurance are based on the financial strength and claims-paying ability of the issuing carrier. That point belongs in the conversation whenever guarantees are discussed.

Planning Perspective

One reason safe money, annuities, and income gaps deserves more space than a quick article or a short seminar comment is that the subject does not stay inside its own lane for very long. A person may begin by asking a straightforward question, then discover that the answer depends on work plans, marital status, spending needs, tax exposure, health concerns, or survivor priorities. That is why a chapter like this is not meant to overwhelm you with detail. It is meant to slow the conversation down enough for the important tradeoffs to become visible.

In real households, this topic usually shows up beside other retirement questions rather than by itself. Someone may be thinking about Whether the household has an income gap before or after claiming Social Security, while also trying to sort out How much of retirement income is already guaranteed versus market-dependent. Another household may be focused on Whether survivor income, long-term care concerns, or legacy goals affect the need for protection-oriented planning and only later realize that Social Security timing is part of the same story. When pieces arrive in that order, the decision can feel more confusing than it really is. Often what is missing is not intelligence. It is simply a calm way to organize the moving parts.

This is also where broad guidance reaches its limit. A chart can teach. A rule of thumb can simplify. An online estimate can point you in the right direction. None of those tools can fully measure what retirement feels like inside one specific household. They do not know how cautious you are, how steady your income needs will be, how one spouse feels compared with the other, or how much flexibility you need if life changes. That is why education is helpful and still not the same thing as personal guidance.

Readers are often relieved when they realize they do not have to solve every part of this alone. You do not need to become your own Social Security office, tax preparer, Medicare analyst, and retirement-income engineer all at once. What you do need is enough understanding to recognize when a decision deserves a wider review. That is a very different goal from trying to self-manage every technical issue from scratch.

A thoughtful review usually changes the tone of the conversation. Instead of asking only, 'What is the biggest number?' people begin asking more useful questions. Which choice protects the household better over time? Which choice fits the way retirement income will actually be used? Which choice respects taxes, Medicare, and survivor concerns instead of discovering them later? Those are not dramatic questions. They are mature planning questions, and they often lead to steadier decisions.

Another reason to revisit this topic carefully is that retirement decisions usually unfold over time rather than all at once. A person may read a chapter like this today, file or delay months from now, and then have to revisit the same ideas after a work change, a health event, a market decline, a Medicare transition, or the loss of a spouse. Good education should still be useful when life moves. That is one reason simple frameworks tend to serve people better than one-time slogans.

It is also worth noticing how often confidence grows when people stop asking for the perfect universal answer and start asking for the right answer for this season of life. The same household may need one strategy at sixty-two, a different strategy at sixty-six, and a different review again after Medicare begins or after one spouse dies. The rules matter, but the calendar of real life matters too. A thoughtful retirement review respects that timing instead of pretending every decision can be made once and ignored forever.

One final point is easy to underestimate: retirement decisions are rarely judged by math alone. They are lived out in monthly routines, family conversations, health changes, and the emotional experience of aging. A strategy that is technically impressive but constantly creates worry may not be the strongest strategy for that household. On the other hand, a strategy that supports steadier habits and clearer expectations may prove more durable over time. That is why practical fit belongs in the conversation right alongside rules and projections.

In that sense, planning around safe money, annuities, and income gaps is not only about information. It is also about alignment. The numbers matter. The rules matter. But the household's values matter too. Some people care deeply about future survivor protection. Some care most about present cash-flow relief. Some want to preserve flexibility because life has already taught them plans can change. A well-guided review makes room for those priorities without letting the conversation drift into guesswork.

That is why the most valuable outcome from this chapter is not memorizing one more rule. The real value is becoming better prepared for a personal review. When you can describe what concerns you, what facts you have, and what tradeoffs matter most, the next conversation becomes more productive. Clarity grows when the discussion moves from a generic topic to your actual retirement picture.

Some households need a way to bridge an income gap or create more predictable income. Safe money strategies and annuity education can be part of that discussion when they are suitable.

These tools have tradeoffs, including liquidity limits, surrender periods, carrier strength, and product design. They should be reviewed carefully, not treated as one-size-fits-all solutions.

Filling the Gap Before a Larger Benefit

Howard wanted to delay Social Security because he liked the idea of a larger future benefit, but he worried about how to cover several years of income in the meantime.

That led to a broader review of savings, withdrawals, and whether a safe money strategy might help reduce anxiety around the bridge period. The answer was not to buy a product first and ask questions later. The answer was to define the planning problem clearly and then evaluate tools that matched it.

Sometimes clarity comes not from choosing a product, but from understanding why a household is even considering one.

Seeking Predictable Income Beyond Social Security

Sharon had Social Security and a modest pension, but she still felt uneasy about how much of her monthly income depended on investments. She wanted to know whether a portion of her assets could be positioned more conservatively to support predictable income later.

That conversation naturally touched on safe money strategies, annuity education, taxes, liquidity, and legacy priorities. It was not a sales pitch. It was a planning conversation about tradeoffs and fit.

When those discussions are done well, the household feels more informed, not pressured.

What People Often Think

People often think Social Security either solves the income problem completely or has nothing to do with the rest of retirement planning. Neither assumption is very helpful.

They also often think annuities should be accepted or rejected in one emotional reaction. In reality, they should be understood as tools that may or may not fit a specific need.

Another common belief is that discussing safe money means abandoning growth altogether. For many households, the real question is balance, not extremes.

What Actually Happens

What actually happens is that some retirees want more guaranteed or more predictable income than Social Security alone provides.

What actually happens is that income gaps, survivor concerns, long-term care concerns, and market stress can all push a household to consider broader protection strategies.

What actually happens is that the best conversations stay educational. They define the problem first, then evaluate whether any safe money or annuity strategy belongs in the plan at all.

Where People Get Stuck

People get stuck because product conversations in the marketplace are often either too aggressive or too shallow.

They also get stuck when they worry that asking about annuities means they are already committing to something. Education should come before commitment.

Another place people struggle is in comparing features without first deciding what the strategy is supposed to accomplish for the household.

What We Typically Review Together

Whether the household has an income gap before or after claiming Social Security.

How much of retirement income is already guaranteed versus market-dependent.

Whether survivor income, long-term care concerns, or legacy goals affect the need for protection-oriented planning.

What role, if any, a safe money or annuity strategy may serve alongside Social Security and other assets.

Liquidity needs, tax considerations, carrier strength considerations, and the tradeoffs involved in any recommended strategy.

Social Security is connected to taxes, Medicare, and retirement income. That connection is worth repeating because it is where many otherwise thoughtful retirees get tripped up. Timing is personal. Online tools are starting points, not final answers. General advice is not the same as personal guidance. Claiming decisions can affect long-term income and survivor planning in ways that are easy to miss when the conversation stays too narrow.

Chapter Summary

Safe money and annuity education belong in the broader retirement income conversation when they solve a real problem, not when they are treated as one-size-fits-all answers.

Social Security timing and broader income planning often work best when they are discussed together.

After looking at the major moving parts, it helps to step back and study the mistakes that commonly derail otherwise thoughtful retirees. The next chapter covers the errors that show up again and again.

Chapter 12: Common Mistakes to Avoid

This chapter matters because many Social Security problems are not caused by lack of intelligence. They are caused by rushing, oversimplifying, or treating one piece of retirement as if it operates alone.

The goal here is not to criticize people. It is to make the common traps easier to recognize before they become expensive.

Simple Explanation

One costly mistake is claiming too early without understanding the long-term tradeoff. Some people file early because it feels natural to start income as soon as it becomes available. In certain households that is appropriate. In others, it permanently reduces a benefit that could have been more valuable later, especially for a spouse who may outlive the higher earner.

Another mistake is waiting too long without a workable income plan. Delaying can strengthen the monthly benefit, but if the bridge years become financially or emotionally unsustainable, the strategy may fail in practice even if it looked good on paper.

Ignoring spouse and survivor effects is another common error. A decision may appear reasonable for one spouse while leaving the surviving spouse with less protection later.

Ignoring taxes and Medicare premium effects also shows up frequently. A household may plan around gross income while overlooking what will actually be kept after taxation and potential IRMAA adjustments.

Relying only on online calculators is another major trap. Calculators can be excellent starting tools. They are not full retirement plans. They do not replace personalized review.

One more mistake is assuming that advice from friends, family, neighbors, or social media applies directly to your life. Their path may be valid for them and still be completely wrong for you.

Finally, many people fail to review the full retirement picture at all. They make the Social Security decision first, then try to patch the rest around it later. That sequence often creates avoidable stress.

Planning Perspective

One reason common mistakes to avoid deserves more space than a quick article or a short seminar comment is that the subject does not stay inside its own lane for very long. A person may begin by asking a straightforward question, then discover that the answer depends on work plans, marital status, spending needs, tax exposure, health concerns, or survivor priorities. That is why a chapter like this is not meant to overwhelm you with detail. It is meant to slow the conversation down enough for the important tradeoffs to become visible.

In real households, this topic usually shows up beside other retirement questions rather than by itself. Someone may be thinking about Whether the current plan claims too early or waits too long without enough context, while also trying to sort out How spouse and survivor income are affected by the chosen filing age. Another household may be focused on Whether taxes, Medicare premiums, and work income have been modeled realistically and only later realize that Social Security timing is part of the same story. When pieces arrive in that order, the decision can feel more confusing than it really is. Often what is missing is not intelligence. It is simply a calm way to organize the moving parts.

This is also where broad guidance reaches its limit. A chart can teach. A rule of thumb can simplify. An online estimate can point you in the right direction. None of those tools can fully measure what retirement feels like inside one specific household. They do not know how cautious you are, how steady your income needs will be, how one spouse feels compared with the other, or how much flexibility you need if life changes. That is why education is helpful and still not the same thing as personal guidance.

Readers are often relieved when they realize they do not have to solve every part of this alone. You do not need to become your own Social Security office, tax preparer, Medicare analyst, and retirement-income engineer all at once. What you do need is enough understanding to recognize when a decision deserves a wider review. That is a very different goal from trying to self-manage every technical issue from scratch.

A thoughtful review usually changes the tone of the conversation. Instead of asking only, 'What is the biggest number?' people begin asking more useful questions. Which choice protects the household better over time? Which choice fits the way retirement income will actually be used? Which choice respects taxes, Medicare, and survivor concerns instead of discovering them later? Those are not dramatic questions. They are mature planning questions, and they often lead to steadier decisions.

Another reason to revisit this topic carefully is that retirement decisions usually unfold over time rather than all at once. A person may read a chapter like this today, file or delay months from now, and then have to revisit the same ideas after a work change, a health event, a market decline, a Medicare transition, or the loss of a spouse. Good education should still be useful when life moves. That is one reason simple frameworks tend to serve people better than one-time slogans.

It is also worth noticing how often confidence grows when people stop asking for the perfect universal answer and start asking for the right answer for this season of life. The same household may need one strategy at sixty-two, a different strategy at sixty-six, and a different review again after Medicare begins or after one spouse dies. The rules matter, but the calendar of real life matters too. A thoughtful retirement review respects that timing instead of pretending every decision can be made once and ignored forever.

One final point is easy to underestimate: retirement decisions are rarely judged by math alone. They are lived out in monthly routines, family conversations, health changes, and the emotional

experience of aging. A strategy that is technically impressive but constantly creates worry may not be the strongest strategy for that household. On the other hand, a strategy that supports steadier habits and clearer expectations may prove more durable over time. That is why practical fit belongs in the conversation right alongside rules and projections.

In that sense, planning around common mistakes to avoid is not only about information. It is also about alignment. The numbers matter. The rules matter. But the household's values matter too. Some people care deeply about future survivor protection. Some care most about present cash-flow relief. Some want to preserve flexibility because life has already taught them plans can change. A well-guided review makes room for those priorities without letting the conversation drift into guesswork.

That is why the most valuable outcome from this chapter is not memorizing one more rule. The real value is becoming better prepared for a personal review. When you can describe what concerns you, what facts you have, and what tradeoffs matter most, the next conversation becomes more productive. Clarity grows when the discussion moves from a generic topic to your actual retirement picture.

Most mistakes are not caused by carelessness. They happen because someone made a decision with only part of the picture visible.

The goal is not to scare the reader. The goal is to help them slow down before turning an avoidable misunderstanding into a permanent retirement decision.

The Early Claim Without Context

Trevor filed as soon as he could because several people told him, 'Take it before the rules change.' He did not review how the lower benefit might affect later survivor income for his wife or how his continued earnings could complicate the picture.

His decision was understandable, but it was under-reviewed. The mistake was not early claiming itself. The mistake was treating urgency as analysis.

A better process would have given him a calm explanation of the tradeoffs before he locked in the choice.

The Delay That Looked Better Than It Felt

Nina delayed because every article she read praised waiting until 70. But the delay forced heavy withdrawals from savings and left her constantly anxious about spending.

On paper, the larger future benefit was attractive. In reality, the household was stretching to maintain the strategy. The problem was not delay itself. The problem was that the plan did not fit her broader financial and emotional comfort zone.

Good planning should be livable.

What People Often Think

People often think mistakes happen only when someone is careless. Many mistakes happen when someone is trying hard to be responsible but is working from incomplete context.

They also often think there is one mistake-free age that would protect everyone from regret. In truth, regret usually comes from not coordinating the choice with the rest of retirement.

Another common belief is that if a strategy sounds logical in isolation, it must be safe overall. That is where many surprises begin.

What Actually Happens

What actually happens is that most costly Social Security mistakes are coordination mistakes. Timing, taxes, Medicare, spouse planning, and income planning were simply not reviewed together.

What actually happens is that households benefit from slowing down long enough to examine the ripple effects of a claiming choice.

What actually happens is that general advice is not the same as personal guidance. That distinction is one of the most valuable protections a retiree can remember.

Where People Get Stuck

People get stuck because they want to avoid regret and therefore search for certainty that does not really exist.

They also get stuck when too many voices compete for attention. A clear review often becomes valuable simply because it reduces noise.

Another place people stall is in waiting until the last minute, when decisions feel rushed and options feel narrower.

What We Typically Review Together

Whether the current plan claims too early or waits too long without enough context.

How spouse and survivor income are affected by the chosen filing age.

Whether taxes, Medicare premiums, and work income have been modeled realistically.

What assumptions are coming from calculators, friends, or headlines rather than from a household review.

Whether the entire retirement income picture has been considered before filing.

Social Security is connected to taxes, Medicare, and retirement income. That connection is worth repeating because it is where many otherwise thoughtful retirees get tripped up. Timing is personal. Online tools are starting points, not final answers. General advice is not the same as personal guidance. Claiming decisions can affect long-term income and survivor planning in ways that are easy to miss when the conversation stays too narrow.

Chapter Summary

Most major mistakes are not about misunderstanding one tiny rule. They are about failing to connect the full picture.

When the whole retirement plan is reviewed, many costly errors become easier to avoid.

Once the common pitfalls are clear, the next helpful step is practical. The next chapter explains what to gather before a review so the conversation can be productive instead of rushed.

Chapter 13: What to Gather Before a Review

This chapter matters because a good review is easier when the right information is gathered ahead of time. Preparation does not have to be complicated, but it does make the conversation more useful.

The purpose of gathering documents is not to make you do all the analysis yourself. It is simply to make sure the discussion starts with clear facts instead of guesses.

Simple Explanation

When people come to a Social Security review with partial numbers or old assumptions, too much time gets spent trying to reconstruct the basics. A little preparation can turn a vague conversation into a clear one.

You do not need a perfect file cabinet or a complete financial binder to begin. Most people simply need the key pieces that show their benefit estimates, retirement timeline, income sources, tax context, and planning concerns.

Gathering these items also helps reveal where the real questions are. Sometimes the most important information is not a document at all, but a concern such as 'I do not want to run out of dependable income' or 'I want to make sure my spouse will be okay if I die first.'

Planning Perspective

One reason what to gather before a review deserves more space than a quick article or a short seminar comment is that the subject does not stay inside its own lane for very long. A person may begin by asking a straightforward question, then discover that the answer depends on work plans, marital status, spending needs, tax exposure, health concerns, or survivor priorities. That is why a chapter like this is not meant to overwhelm you with detail. It is meant to slow the conversation down enough for the important tradeoffs to become visible.

In real households, this topic usually shows up beside other retirement questions rather than by itself. Someone may be thinking about Your current Social Security statement or online benefit estimate, while also trying to sort out Spouse information and the spouse's Social Security estimate, if applicable. Another household may be focused on An estimate of retirement income needs and the planned retirement date and only later realize that Social Security timing is part of the same story. When pieces arrive in that order, the decision can feel more confusing than it really is. Often what is missing is not intelligence. It is simply a calm way to organize the moving parts.

This is also where broad guidance reaches its limit. A chart can teach. A rule of thumb can simplify. An online estimate can point you in the right direction. None of those tools can fully measure what retirement feels like inside one specific household. They do not know how cautious you are, how steady your income needs will be, how one spouse feels compared with the other, or how much flexibility you need if life changes. That is why education is helpful and still not the same thing as personal guidance.

Readers are often relieved when they realize they do not have to solve every part of this alone. You do not need to become your own Social Security office, tax preparer, Medicare analyst, and retirement-income engineer all at once. What you do need is enough understanding to recognize when a decision deserves a wider review. That is a very different goal from trying to self-manage every technical issue from scratch.

A thoughtful review usually changes the tone of the conversation. Instead of asking only, 'What is the biggest number?' people begin asking more useful questions. Which choice protects the household better over time? Which choice fits the way retirement income will actually be used? Which choice respects taxes, Medicare, and survivor concerns instead of discovering them later? Those are not dramatic questions. They are mature planning questions, and they often lead to steadier decisions.

Another reason to revisit this topic carefully is that retirement decisions usually unfold over time rather than all at once. A person may read a chapter like this today, file or delay months from now, and then have to revisit the same ideas after a work change, a health event, a market decline, a Medicare transition, or the loss of a spouse. Good education should still be useful when life moves. That is one reason simple frameworks tend to serve people better than one-time slogans.

It is also worth noticing how often confidence grows when people stop asking for the perfect universal answer and start asking for the right answer for this season of life. The same household may need one strategy at sixty-two, a different strategy at sixty-six, and a different review again after Medicare begins or after one spouse dies. The rules matter, but the calendar of real life matters too. A thoughtful retirement review respects that timing instead of pretending every decision can be made once and ignored forever.

One final point is easy to underestimate: retirement decisions are rarely judged by math alone. They are lived out in monthly routines, family conversations, health changes, and the emotional experience of aging. A strategy that is technically impressive but constantly creates worry may not be the strongest strategy for that household. On the other hand, a strategy that supports steadier habits and clearer expectations may prove more durable over time. That is why practical fit belongs in the conversation right alongside rules and projections.

In that sense, planning around what to gather before a review is not only about information. It is also about alignment. The numbers matter. The rules matter. But the household's values matter too. Some people care deeply about future survivor protection. Some care most about present cash-flow relief. Some want to preserve flexibility because life has already taught them plans can change. A well-guided review makes room for those priorities without letting the conversation drift into guesswork.

That is why the most valuable outcome from this chapter is not memorizing one more rule. The real value is becoming better prepared for a personal review. When you can describe what concerns you, what facts you have, and what tradeoffs matter most, the next conversation becomes more productive. Clarity grows when the discussion moves from a generic topic to your actual retirement picture.

Good information makes a better review. A client does not need to know every answer, but bringing the right documents helps the conversation move from general education into personal clarity.

This chapter works best as a preparation tool. It helps the reader come organized without making them feel like they have to solve the planning issues alone.

A Review That Started With Good Facts

Brenda brought her Social Security statement, her husband's estimate, a simple list of retirement accounts, pension details, and a rough monthly income target. That preparation did not solve the decision by itself, but it made the conversation far more productive.

Instead of spending the appointment guessing, the review could focus on timing tradeoffs, taxes, survivor issues, and next steps. Good preparation created better questions.

This is often the difference between a generic conversation and a meaningful one.

A Review Built on Memory Alone

Calvin came in with strong opinions about when he should claim, but most of the supporting details were estimates he remembered from old statements or conversations.

Once current documents were gathered, the picture looked different enough that his original confidence started to soften. The issue was not that he had done anything wrong. The issue was that the plan deserved better information.

That is why preparation is not busywork. It protects the quality of the conversation.

What People Often Think

People often think they need every document from every account before they can ask for help. That is usually not necessary.

Others think they can remember the important numbers well enough. Sometimes they can, but too often one missing detail changes the conversation.

Another common belief is that if the Social Security statement is available online, that is the only document that matters. It is an important starting point, not the whole picture.

What Actually Happens

What actually helps most is gathering the core items that shape the claiming decision and the broader retirement plan.

What actually happens is that a better-prepared review can spend less time reconstructing facts and more time evaluating options.

What actually matters is not perfect organization. It is enough clarity to support a thoughtful discussion.

Where People Get Stuck

People get stuck because paperwork feels overwhelming.

They also get stuck when one spouse knows where the documents are and the other does not. That can delay important conversations.

Another place people struggle is in assuming they need to understand every document before bringing it to a review. In reality, part of the value of a review is helping interpret what matters.

What We Typically Review Together

Your current Social Security statement or online benefit estimate.

Spouse information and the spouse's Social Security estimate, if applicable.

An estimate of retirement income needs and the planned retirement date.

Pension statements or pension estimates.

Retirement account information such as IRA, 401(k), 403(b), or similar balances.

Current Medicare status or expected Medicare timing.

Tax filing status and a rough sense of taxable income sources.

Any planned work income in retirement.

Questions, concerns, goals, and anything that makes the decision feel difficult.

Social Security is connected to taxes, Medicare, and retirement income. That connection is worth repeating because it is where many otherwise thoughtful retirees get tripped up. Timing is personal. Online tools are starting points, not final answers. General advice is not the same as personal guidance. Claiming decisions can affect long-term income and survivor planning in ways that are easy to miss when the conversation stays too narrow.

Chapter Summary

Preparation does not mean doing the planning alone. It simply gives the review a stronger foundation.

When the right information is gathered, the Social Security conversation becomes more focused, more personal, and more useful.

Once the facts are assembled, the final step is learning how to think through the decision with confidence. The next chapter offers a practical framework for making that choice without pretending it is one-size-fits-all.

Chapter 14: Making a Confident Decision

This chapter matters because the goal of all this education is not to leave you with more information but less clarity. The point is to help you make a decision with more confidence and less noise.

Confidence does not mean pretending the future is fully predictable. It means choosing a path that fits your household after the most important factors have been reviewed.

Simple Explanation

A useful decision framework begins with the benefit estimates at different ages, but it does not stop there. Next, look at income needs. How much dependable income is needed now, and how much may be needed later?

Then consider the household context. Are you single or married? Is one spouse's benefit likely to matter more for survivor income? Will one spouse keep working? Are there pensions, retirement accounts, or safe money strategies that change the pressure on Social Security timing?

After that, review taxes and Medicare. A claiming choice that looks attractive on paper may feel different after income taxes, premium changes, and withdrawal sequencing are taken into account.

Then look at emotional fit. Does the strategy support peace of mind, or does it create a plan that the household will resent or struggle to follow? Good planning should be realistic enough to live with.

Finally, ask whether the decision still makes sense when viewed from the survivor perspective, not just the retiree's perspective. That question alone improves many decisions.

Planning Perspective

One reason making a confident decision deserves more space than a quick article or a short seminar comment is that the subject does not stay inside its own lane for very long. A person may begin by asking a straightforward question, then discover that the answer depends on work plans, marital status, spending needs, tax exposure, health concerns, or survivor priorities. That is why a chapter like this is not meant to overwhelm you with detail. It is meant to slow the conversation down enough for the important tradeoffs to become visible.

In real households, this topic usually shows up beside other retirement questions rather than by itself. Someone may be thinking about the estimated benefits at key filing ages, while also trying to sort out Current and future income needs. Another household may be focused on Spouse and survivor considerations and only later realize that Social Security timing is part of the same story. When pieces arrive in that order, the decision can feel more confusing than it really is. Often what is missing is not intelligence. It is simply a calm way to organize the moving parts.

This is also where broad guidance reaches its limit. A chart can teach. A rule of thumb can simplify. An online estimate can point you in the right direction. None of those tools can fully measure what retirement feels like inside one specific household. They do not know how cautious you are, how steady your income needs will be, how one spouse feels compared with the other, or how much flexibility you need if life changes. That is why education is helpful and still not the same thing as personal guidance.

Readers are often relieved when they realize they do not have to solve every part of this alone. You do not need to become your own Social Security office, tax preparer, Medicare analyst, and retirement-income engineer all at once. What you do need is enough understanding to recognize when a decision deserves a wider review. That is a very different goal from trying to self-manage every technical issue from scratch.

A thoughtful review usually changes the tone of the conversation. Instead of asking only, 'What is the biggest number?' people begin asking more useful questions. Which choice protects the household better over time? Which choice fits the way retirement income will actually be used? Which choice respects taxes, Medicare, and survivor concerns instead of discovering them later? Those are not dramatic questions. They are mature planning questions, and they often lead to steadier decisions.

Another reason to revisit this topic carefully is that retirement decisions usually unfold over time rather than all at once. A person may read a chapter like this today, file or delay months from now, and then have to revisit the same ideas after a work change, a health event, a market decline, a Medicare transition, or the loss of a spouse. Good education should still be useful when life moves. That is one reason simple frameworks tend to serve people better than one-time slogans.

It is also worth noticing how often confidence grows when people stop asking for the perfect universal answer and start asking for the right answer for this season of life. The same household may need one strategy at sixty-two, a different strategy at sixty-six, and a different review again after Medicare begins or after one spouse dies. The rules matter, but the calendar of real life matters too. A thoughtful retirement review respects that timing instead of pretending every decision can be made once and ignored forever.

One final point is easy to underestimate: retirement decisions are rarely judged by math alone. They are lived out in monthly routines, family conversations, health changes, and the emotional experience of aging. A strategy that is technically impressive but constantly creates worry may not be the strongest strategy for that household. On the other hand, a strategy that supports steadier habits and clearer expectations may prove more durable over time. That is why practical fit belongs in the conversation right alongside rules and projections.

In that sense, planning around making a confident decision is not only about information. It is also about alignment. The numbers matter. The rules matter. But the household's values matter too. Some people care deeply about future survivor protection. Some care most about present cash-flow relief. Some want to preserve flexibility because life has already taught them plans can change. A well-guided review makes room for those priorities without letting the conversation drift into guesswork.

That is why the most valuable outcome from this chapter is not memorizing one more rule. The real value is becoming better prepared for a personal review. When you can describe what concerns you, what facts you have, and what tradeoffs matter most, the next conversation becomes more productive. Clarity grows when the discussion moves from a generic topic to your actual retirement picture.

Confidence does not mean having every rule memorized. It means understanding the major tradeoffs and knowing the decision has been reviewed in context.

A good decision framework should organize the conversation, not replace it. The goal is better questions, better facts, and a clearer next step.

Choosing Confidence Over Guesswork

Diane wanted someone to simply tell her the right age to claim. Instead, she was guided through a framework that connected benefit estimates, work, taxes, Medicare, survivor planning, and cash flow.

At first, that felt like more information than she wanted. In the end, it gave her something better than a quick opinion. It gave her confidence in why the decision fit her life.

That is often the real goal. Most people are not looking for more complexity. They are looking for grounded clarity.

A Couple Reaching a Shared Decision

Eric wanted immediate income. Paula wanted stronger long-term protection. Their conversations kept circling because they were arguing from different priorities.

Once they used a review framework that acknowledged both current cash flow and future survivor concerns, the tension lowered. They were no longer defending positions. They were comparing tradeoffs.

That shift made the final decision feel shared rather than imposed.

What People Often Think

People often think confidence comes from finding one magic rule.

Others think confidence should feel like complete certainty. Retirement decisions rarely work that way.

Another common belief is that if a choice still has tradeoffs, it must be the wrong choice. Most good decisions still involve tradeoffs. The point is to choose the tradeoff that fits.

What Actually Happens

What actually creates confidence is understanding the main moving parts and seeing how they apply to your household.

What actually helps is knowing that online tools are useful starting points, but final decisions should be grounded in personal guidance and the broader retirement picture.

What actually works is a decision framework that respects both the numbers and the people living with them.

Where People Get Stuck

People get stuck when they think confidence should arrive before the review instead of through it.

They also get stuck when they keep reopening the question after every new article or opinion they hear.

Another place people stall is in fearing regret so much that they postpone the decision longer than necessary.

What We Typically Review Together

The estimated benefits at key filing ages.

Current and future income needs.

Spouse and survivor considerations.

Taxes, Medicare, work income, and withdrawal strategy.

Emotional comfort, flexibility needs, and broader protection goals.

Social Security is connected to taxes, Medicare, and retirement income. That connection is worth repeating because it is where many otherwise thoughtful retirees get tripped up. Timing is personal. Online tools are starting points, not final answers. General advice is not the same as personal guidance. Claiming decisions can affect long-term income and survivor planning in ways that are easy to miss when the conversation stays too narrow.

Chapter Summary

A confident Social Security decision does not come from a slogan. It comes from a framework.

The more clearly the decision is tied to your full retirement picture, the more confidence most households feel.

The remaining chapters pull this education into practical next steps, including how a review can be structured and how broader retirement conversations may connect around Social Security, Medicare, and protection planning.

Chapter 15: How Price Services Group Can Help

This book is designed to help you understand the key issues before you make a Social Security decision. It is not designed to replace a personal review.

Price Services Group, L.L.C. helps clients look at Social Security in context with the rest of their retirement picture. Depending on your situation, a review may include:

Social Security timing conversations

Medicare plan reviews

Retirement income planning conversations

Safe money strategy discussions

Annuity education and retirement income discussions

Life insurance reviews

Long-term care planning discussions

Legacy and protection planning conversations

Medicare-related and non-Medicare planning conversations may need to be handled separately depending on the products and issues being discussed.

Your Next Step

If you would like help reviewing how Social Security fits into your broader retirement picture, you can schedule a personalized review.

Website: priceservicesgroup.com

Medicare education/class: learnmedicare.org/home

Booking: host.safemsngr.com/widget/bookings/psgss

Chapter 16: About the Author

Kayla Price is a licensed insurance professional and attorney who helps individuals, families, and business owners make clearer decisions about insurance, Medicare, Social Security, retirement planning, life insurance, safe money strategies, and broader protection planning.

Through Price Services Group, L.L.C., she focuses on helping clients worry less by making complex decisions easier to understand. Her work centers on practical education, calmer conversations, and helping clients see how one decision often affects several others.

Kayla's approach is straightforward: give people enough clarity to ask better questions, then help them review their options in context instead of relying on guesswork, headlines, or one-size-fits-all advice.

Nothing in this book, and no review described in it, creates an attorney-client relationship unless separately agreed in writing.

Bring This Book to Your Review

Bring this book with you to your Social Security review appointment. If you marked pages, wrote questions, or circled sections that felt important, we can use those notes to make the conversation more personal and productive.

Chapter 17: Annual Update Note

This 2026 edition is intended to be reviewed annually. Social Security figures, Medicare premiums, IRMAA thresholds, taxable wage bases, earnings-test limits, tax references, and planning considerations may change from year to year.

Even when the general rules stay familiar, the numbers that affect real households can shift. Annual review helps keep the book accurate and helps prevent an old assumption from driving a new decision.

Annual Review Checklist

Each year, consider reviewing:

- ☐ Social Security benefit estimates and earnings records

  COLA and annual Social Security figures

  Earnings-test limits

  Taxable wage base

  Medicare Part B premium and deductible references

- ☐ IRMAA thresholds and income brackets
- ☐ Tax references related to Social Security and retirement withdrawals
- ☐ Spousal, survivor, divorce, remarriage, WEP/GPO, or government pension updates
- ☐ Booking link and contact information
- ☐ Disclaimer and non-affiliation language

Final Thought

Social Security is important, but it is only one part of retirement planning. The stronger question is not simply, "When should I claim?" It is, "How does this decision fit into the life I am trying to build and protect?"

When you are ready, review your situation before making a final decision.

Price Services Group, L.L.C. | priceservicesgroup.com | Social Security Review: https://host.safemsngr.com/widget/bookings/psgss